"A beautiful, joyous book that will only take a day to read—and yet, Mike Fairclough says such wise and wonderful things it could change your life forever."

DAME JACQUELINE WILSON,
BEST-SELLING CHILDREN'S AUTHOR

"This marvelous little book pretends with its brevity to be lightweight but punches so far above it that it makes you see stars. A fizzing, personal journey of self-discovery that opens a box of tricks on how to be present, happy and capable of wonder. Its main message is the wisdom of the ages: 'Rules are for the guidance of the wise and the enslavement of the stupid,' a paean to playfulness, a celebration of the guiding light of our imagination, and how to set it on fire once more—a little classic."

SIR TIM SMIT, BEST-SELLING AUTHOR AND
CO-FOUNDER OF THE EDEN PROJECT

"Simply the best book on creativity and the proper use of imagination I have ever read. Warm, tempting, and insightful, it has powerfully touched my soul."

MIKE DOOLEY, *NEW YORK TIMES* BESTSELLING
AUTHOR OF *INFINITE POSSIBILITIES*

"*I was captivated from the first paragraph. I was the child whose imagination was set loose by something she has seen out of the classroom window. Wild Thing is easy to read, full of personal stories and useful tips for the reader to follow, to recapture the magic, optimism, and joyful appreciation of childhood.*"

SARAH, DUCHESS OF YORK

"*This is a beautiful, life-affirming book; inspiring, provocative, joyous, and accessible. Mike Fairclough is a remarkable and a visionary human being who has made it his life's mission to bring happiness to adults and children alike through reconnecting us all to the wonders and possibilities of the world around us.*"

RICHARD GERVER,
AWARD-WINNING SPEAKER AND BEST-SELLING AUTHOR

"*Mike Fairclough's fresh and intensely personal book is liberating from start to finish. He uses his life, gathering wisdom and experience in running a highly successful school, to provide teachers and learners with permission to be their most human selves. On a journey rich with key autobiographical stories, Mike leads us to rediscover the joy and playfulness that release creativity, imagination, and the capacity to be the best people we can be.*"

DR. JONATHAN BARNES, BEST-SELLING AUTHOR

"Mike Fairclough is doing something magical at West Rise Junior School—magic that has drawn the eyes of educators from around the world. Wild Thing *explains the magic in a way you can bring it into your life, no matter your age. Relax, read, and rejuvenate with* Wild Thing—*it'll spark forgotten creativity that still lies within."*

PROFESSOR BARBARA OAKLEY,
NEW YORK TIMES BEST-SELLING AUTHOR

"A must-read for anyone working in the creative industries. Mike Fairclough's brilliant Wild Thing *will take you on a deliciously playful adventure, helping you reconnect with the carefree child you once were so you can claim the blissful life you deserve."*

EMILIA DI GIROLAMO, SHOWRUNNER AND SCREENWRITER

"I enjoyed reading this book. Challenging myself with 'if we can see the potential, the mystery and the magic in every moment . . .' Not instantly easy for a politician and a businessman! Still, by the end, perhaps I shall have proved Monty Python's song right (It's fun to charter an accountant, and sail the wide accountancy). I feel the tide lifting my old hull already!"

LORD LUCAS, 12TH BARON LUCAS AND 8TH LORD DINGWALL; HEREDITARY PEER IN THE HOUSE OF LORDS

WILD THING

WILD THING

**Embracing Childhood Traits in Adulthood
for a Happier, More Carefree Life**

MIKE FAIRCLOUGH

HAY HOUSE

Carlsbad, California • New York City
London • Sydney • New Delhi

Published in the United Kingdom by:
Hay House UK Ltd, The Sixth Floor, Watson House,
54 Baker Street, London W1U 7BU
Tel: +44 (0)20 3927 7290; Fax: +44 (0)20 3927 7291; www.hayhouse.co.uk

Published in the United States of America by:
Hay House Inc., PO Box 5100, Carlsbad, CA 92018-5100
Tel: (1) 760 431 7695 or (800) 654 5126
Fax: (1) 760 431 6948 or (800) 650 5115; www.hayhouse.com

Published in Australia by:
Hay House Australia Pty Ltd, 18/36 Ralph St, Alexandria NSW 2015
Tel: (61) 2 9669 4299; Fax: (61) 2 9669 4144; www.hayhouse.com.au

Published in India by:
Hay House Publishers India, Muskaan Complex,
Plot No.3, B-2, Vasant Kunj, New Delhi 110 070
Tel: (91) 11 4176 1620; Fax: (91) 11 4176 1630; www.hayhouse.co.in

A catalogue record for this book is available from the British Library.

Tradepaper ISBN: 978-1-78817-628-6
E-book ISBN: 978-1-78817-629-3
Audiobook ISBN: 978-1-78817-630-9

Interior images: Shutterstock

Printed and bound by CPI Group (UK) Ltd, Croydon, CR0 4YY

To my rock 'n' roll wife, Sundeep Sitara, and our magical children, Tali, Iggy, Luna, and Star.

May we always be wild things.

CONTENTS

INTRODUCTION

We all remember times in childhood when we were sitting in a classroom. The teacher was introducing the lesson and we were completely engaged and attentive. Then something caught our eye out of the window, or a thought came into our mind. Suddenly, we were in another world.

This introduction is brief as I don't want to lose your attention. And yet, somewhere within those childhood wonderings of the mind is a gift for us in adulthood.

I have had children of my own and taught other people's children for over 20 years and strongly believe that they have powerful and transformative insights that can teach us all something indispensable about life. Just look at how happy most of them are. Of course, they don't pay the bills or have the weight of the world on their shoulders. But is that the real reason for their happiness?

Children are rapidly evolving beings who face enormous challenges. They first have to learn to walk and to talk. Then, they have to work out the complexities of their first social relationships and engage with the adult world. All children regularly have to step out of their comfort zones, build grit and resilience, and develop their physical, emotional, and mental capacities at a great pace. The equivalent in the adult world would be if we had to learn to fly within a matter of weeks or months.

How do children face such challenges, yet remain so happy, elated, even ecstatic?

Their secret is Imagination.

We often attribute the world of imagination to children, but imagination is also responsible for every major human success story—from the creation of writing and music to the development of the arts. It is responsible for the conception of human societies and is the source of every technological advancement throughout history. It has the power to enrich relationships and create success at work.

Imagination is a powerful force that transforms lives. And children are masters when it comes to using it.

Wild Thing is about reclaiming our imagination and rekindling our enthusiasm for life. It is an invitation for us to explore and play . . . to be wild and free.

Together, we will reignite the lost art of living imaginatively and see that our childlike enthusiasm and lust for life never really died. It has just been waiting for us to rediscover it.

Do I still have your attention? Yes? Then let's go!

1

BORN TO BE WILD

I remember feeling invincible, coupled with a sensation of imminent danger, and I loved it. Clinging to the top branch of the tallest tree in my back garden, its trunk bending impossibly with each new gust of wind, I had previously been watching the ominous black clouds advancing toward my bedroom window. The irresistible urge to go outside had consumed me. Now, at the storm's exhilarating peak, I hung by one arm from the tree while reaching out to the sky with the other, hoping to seize the very essence of the lightning flash as it arced above me. I became a wizard, summoning the energy of the storm. And with the next crack of thunder, I was a Cherokee Indian, heroically surveying the terrain from my lookout post and battling against the elements.

I became these characters in my seven-year-old imagination, but the storm was very real. To this day, the clarity of that memory is evoked every time I climb a tree, and I still cannot resist going outside in a storm.

Like my seven-year-old younger self, the same enthusiasm for life and feeling excited and elated flows effortlessly through all children. I have seen it in the hundreds of children who I have taught over my career in education spanning over 25 years. I also believe that harnessing this same enthusiasm for life is at the heart of the emotional well-being of adults. If only we can recapture it.

Reigniting Our Passion for Life

*"We don't stop playing because we grow old;
we grow old because we stop playing."*
GEORGE BERNARD SHAW

When we watch children play, we can see that this is how they begin to learn about the world around them. The skills they acquire and the states of mind they adopt eventually help them to navigate their way through the inevitable ups and downs of life. I feel like my numerous childhood adventures in nature—generally in my back garden—have given me a sense of resilience and a temptation to seek out fun in later life. When I was eventually allowed to venture out beyond my garden at the age of ten, my friends and I would play in the local fields, farms, and hills in Buckinghamshire, where we lived. This is where we learnt to explore hidden places and where we had great fun breaking various rules. Again, what seemed like a playful adventure to us at the time set us up with particular traits and skills for adult life.

I believe that if we can cultivate the same level of awe and wonder for life that children have, and if we can see the potential, the mystery, and the magic in every moment, then our adult lives will be completely transformed. We just need to ignite that inner fire and passion for life, which we felt so abundantly when we were children. On the surface, this might sound like a difficult or even impossible ambition, but it is actually surprisingly easy to achieve. And the path to us getting there is both rewarding and fun.

Playfulness and the Spirit of Adventure

"We are never more fully alive, more completely ourselves, or more deeply engrossed in anything than when we are playing."

CHARLES SCHAEFER

I think that my memory of climbing the tree as a boy is so vivid because I embraced the moment. Of course, it was ridiculously dangerous and definitely wild, but there is something about seizing the moment in the way that children do so easily that we can observe and learn from. Children's natural disposition to live in the present encourages them to seek out enjoyable experiences, which they then engage in on a deep emotional and physical level. They are much less concerned with the past or the future than adults are. Having observed the behaviors of my pupils over the years, I have come to the realization that they possess two very important qualities that help them to be in the present moment and to regularly feel emotions such as joy and elation. The first of these qualities is "the spirit of adventure." Children seek out new experiences while they are playing and are delighted to embrace the unknown. Life is an adventure to them, and they embrace it wholeheartedly. The second and equally important trait is one that we often associate with children—all of them portray the magical quality of "playfulness." A child who is playful is one who is light-hearted, creative, and imaginative. Playfulness is really at the heart of every child. It is an attitude toward life in general and the motivation behind their games and pursuits.

Why shouldn't adults, too, enjoy having a spirit of adventure and adopt a playful attitude toward life? These qualities bring with them such positive and transformative benefits to mind, body, and emotional well-being. Engaging with the world creatively, seeking out new experiences, and witnessing the magic and wonder in the world around us makes us feel upbeat and excited about our lives and what is in store for us. This, in turn, is integral to our feelings of sustainable and deep happiness. If only we could give ourselves "permission" to embrace these powerful traits within us, they would become our trusted allies and valuable tools.

Evoking these traits becomes easy when we accept that the spirit of adventure and playfulness are simply natural states of being. They are just like breathing, eating, thinking, and sleeping. And cultivating them isn't a long-drawn-out process, either. You can ignite playfulness and adventure in your lives today.

First, it might be helpful to remember what it was like to be a child. Let us cast our minds back for a moment to when we were children and were busy enjoying imaginative games and play. What memories and sensations from childhood adventures can be evoked? While remembering, we may begin to experience a fluttering in our heart and a lightness in our bodies. What other physical sensations and emotions can be felt? Perhaps there are visual pictures or films that can be replayed in our mind. It might simply be a flicker, or sensation of memory, that we are able to detect. Spending a bit of time remembering what it was like to be playful and adventurous as a child may help us in looking at the world with our rose-tinted glasses, which will help us throughout our journey. Immersing ourselves in positive memories every now and then is quite enjoyable as well.

The Importance of Imagination

*"Logic will take you from A to B. Imagination
will take you everywhere."*

ALBERT EINSTEIN

We are going to be playful, carefree, and adventurous throughout this book and beyond. The process of enhancing our well-being and enjoyment of life is not dependent on our past. It is about enjoying our life today and looking forward with excitement and enthusiasm to our future. Whether we can remember much from our childhood or not, rekindling a playful approach to adult life is surprisingly quick and easy. We were all born to be wild, regardless of our age, background, or belief. There were numerous occasions when we felt carefree, euphoric, and invincible when we were younger, and we can feel this same way again. Imagination can take us anywhere and help us to break free from the shackles of everyday life and sprinkle a pinch of joy and bliss to it.

A child's natural state of being is to smile and laugh, and they are instinctively drawn to whatever makes them feel happy. We all began life this way. It's just that, somewhere along our life's journey, an adult, or an institution of adults, told us that we shouldn't feel like this anymore. We were told that we were being "childish" or "not serious enough" and made to feel that being playful and adventurous was a waste of our time. These sorts of negative messages are unhelpful, and it is good to begin to release them. We all have a right to feel free and enjoy our existence. Life doesn't need to be an endurance test, nor should it be taken too seriously. Life is a precious gift that is meant to be enjoyed.

At the root of having a spirit of adventure and a sense of playfulness about the world is imagination. Imagination is the key component to this way of living and most children are absolutely brimming with it. They appear to step effortlessly into alternative realities, where they are able to become any character that they choose to be. We have all seen children take on the mantle of a superhero, princess, soldier, wizard, or sportsperson, among other infinite roles. They can also seamlessly flit from one character to another, altering their posture, movements, and voices to suit the role. We may have also seen children invent games out of thin air; adhering to rules and parameters, which then evolve as the game progresses. This creative activity is always fluid and rarely fixed. If it doesn't work, the rules, or characters, are changed instantly. As long as it feels expansive and fun, children are happy to experiment and play. For us adults, the spirit of adventure and playfulness invites us to adopt a more fluid and flexible approach to our lives, and it is our imagination, in particular, which is our most powerful and transformative asset in order to achieve this. We simply need to keep an open mind, relax, and enjoy the process.

When it comes to imagination, the sky is the limit, and one doesn't need to be a certain age to think or daydream beyond daily life.

You Are Already More Playful Than You Think

"If you fall in love with the imagination,
you understand that it is a free spirit.
It will go anywhere, and it can do anything."
ALICE WALKER

If cultivating these traits sounds a bit tricky, it is good to remember that happy states of consciousness, a playful attitude to life, and having a spirit of adventure occur in our current lives already, however fleetingly. We may have felt playful while dancing at a party or when we have connected with an old friend and recollected memories from the past. It is likely that we feel childlike states of consciousness in adult life more often than we fully appreciate. Another example of this is when we have read a book, or watched a film, and secretly identified with the main character. We may have momentarily adopted the way they look or the way they walk and repeated a catchphrase used by the character. I used to think that I was the only adult I knew who did this, but once I began to ask others whether they do the same thing, they all told me that they, too, "play" in this way. When we have mimicked even the smallest traits of another character, we have role-played in the way that children do but with more subtlety and, probably, hoping that no one else has noticed us. The point being, at these times, we are using our imagination and being playful.

Is it a waste of time indulging our imagination in this way? Not at all. The positive physical and emotional reactions we have, when our minds are engaged in this kind of activity, are great for our overall well-being. Feeling even a flicker of positive emotions is extremely beneficial to our general health and sense of happiness. The trick is to sustain these uplifting feelings as they, along with imagination, can help us to achieve a sense of bliss.

Another playful phenomenon, common to every child, and that we all engage in, is daydreaming. This is where we imagine ourselves in different contexts, often replaying events and changing the setting to suit our mood. This is a natural process, which, like children, we use to practice future scenarios or to reframe past events. How many times have we replayed a past experience and changed the outcome to one that we preferred? Or imagined future events and played out various storylines in our mind's eye, practicing and rehearsing a multitude of responses and imagined outcomes?

It is important to avoid daydreams that cause us to feel negative emotions such as anger, sadness, or jealousy. This only serves to make us feel unhappy and anxious and that, in turn, can be detrimental to our physical well-being. We know how we feel in our bodies when we are angry or sad, so avoiding triggers for these feelings is a good idea. Negative thinking can also become addictive, and it can lead to unwanted outcomes in the real world. In order to enhance our positive emotions, we are invited to commit to using our imagination for positive thoughts and visualizations alone. When we imagine an enjoyable experience, our emotional and physical reaction is instant.

Not only does this feel good, but it can also help us to achieve our goals.

For some people, daydreaming wasn't seen in a positive light by the adults around them in childhood. We may have been told to "stop daydreaming" and to get our head "out of the clouds" among other negative messages. None of these statements is helpful to us in adult life. Our imagination is one of our most treasured tools and daydreaming is a beneficial and enjoyable pursuit. It can make us feel extremely positive and is able to enhance our playful and adventurous outlook on life. It is also a great way to experiment with future and positive scenarios, and it is a way of imagining future realities for ourselves. If we spend some of our time imagining the life of our dreams, we are far more likely to achieve it.

Embracing the Unknown

*"I'm very good at daydreaming.
Ask any of my schoolteachers."*

Bruce Dickinson

Daydreaming becomes even more enjoyable when we embrace the unknown. Wouldn't it be fantastic to become explorers, both in the real world and within our inner realities? The more magical and mysterious the uncharted route, the better. Again, curiosity may have been seen as a dangerous concept by some adults and institutions in our early lives, often preferring to be more cautious and to stick to known paths. After all, we have been told that "curiosity killed the cat." The trouble with that approach is that life is not the same for everybody, we don't all tread on the same path, and we are constantly having to deal with unforeseeable situations. Telling ourselves and our children to fear the unknown is not preparing them, or ourselves, for the reality of existence. It also misses the magic and possibility hidden within the unknown.

When we struggle with unpredictable circumstances, we begin to fear them. This can cause anxiety and make us resort to freezing or giving a fight-or-flight response to events that we perceive to be out of our control. This occurs when we view life as dangerous, instead of seeing it as an opportunity . . . as magical and exciting. Approaching life in a more carefree and playful manner, in the way that children naturally do, will help us to cope more easily with events in our daily lives. There will be lots of times when we feel out of our depth and in unfamiliar terrain, but we can see this as an inevitable part of life and as an opportunity for us to learn and grow. This may sound overly simplistic, but it really is our choice. As children, we naturally embraced the mystery of life, but due to the messages we may have received years ago from others who feared it, we grew to fear it, too.

The Power of Your Imagination

"Imagination will often carry us to worlds that never were. But without it we go nowhere."
CARL SAGAN

Author and speaker Sir Ken Robinson was a great advocate of the principles we are beginning to explore within this book. I first heard him speak at an education conference on the subject of creativity about 10 years ago. The backdrop to his speech was a panoramic view of the Brighton coastline, close to where I live and work. The spectacle of the glistening sea was certainly magnificent, but the subject of Sir Ken's talk, "Do schools kill creativity?" was what really took my breath away. He said, "Imagination is the source of every form of human achievement." A powerful statement indeed. And when we look at the world around us, it is easy to agree with this idea. Even more exciting for us is that the imagination is a gift that we all possess, albeit, at times, as an underused asset. Sir Ken went on to say that imagination is "the one thing that I believe we are systematically jeopardizing in the way we educate our children and ourselves." He described how governments and educational establishments around the world have been stifling creativity and imagination for decades. This is largely because they have been operating on an outdated model of education, dating back to the Industrial Age. These systems, which are deeply rooted in conformity and control, and heavily weighted on learning *facts* rather than acquiring *skills*, were relevant in the 1800s, but this method isn't relevant anymore. Sir Ken also argued that it is vital that our approach to education and creativity evolves in order for society to progress and for individuals to reach their full potential.

For me, one of the best examples of someone who has harnessed the power of their imagination is my father-in-law, Professor Sital Singh Sitara MBE. Now in his 80s, he finally moved to London in 1975 after moving to East Africa from India. At the age of three, he went completely blind in both eyes due to a rare virus. At that point, it was assumed that he would live a life of high dependency on others and would struggle to find work and never have a family of his own. However, Sital was a boy with an extraordinarily strong imagination and a dream to become a musician. He longed to perform on stage, and, once he became a teenager, he had the vision to teach music to others. So began years of tremendous hard work as he learnt Indian classical instruments such as the violin, harmonium, sitar, and tabla. Not only did he achieve all of this in the face of physical adversity, but he also learnt, by heart, the entire Sikh holy book, Guru Granth Sahib.

On arriving in London, and not speaking a word of English, he cultivated a new vision. His plan was to bring Indian classical and religious music to his new home and to open Sikh temples across the UK. Over the following 40 years, he did just that. Traveling alone and without the aid of a guide dog or human assistance, Sital learnt the complete map of the London Underground. He used his imagination to create his own map in his mind, which, to this day, he uses to navigate his way across the complex, and often disrupted, transport system. He has since founded and co-founded many Sikh temples and taught Indian music to three generations of British Asians—close to 20,000 people. When I first met him and learnt that Sital had also authored three books, created albums of his music, founded a charity for blind children in India, and fathered three children, I asked him how he had achieved so much. He told me that his blindness was not an obstacle for him and that he had an "inner vision" that guided and inspired him.

This inner vision enables him to write his own poetry, compose his own music, and teach the skills of classical Indian instruments and religious songs to others. Sital's inner vision is a vivid example of imagination in its purest and most potent form. Today, he continues to teach every day of the week, prolifically create new work, and come up with fresh ideas. His imagination and willpower have influenced England's rich cultural landscape, enhanced the lives of others, and made his own life a complete success.

Human Resources Are Like Natural Resources

"Imagination is the beginning of creation.
You imagine what you desire, you will what you
imagine and at last you create what you will."
GEORGE BERNARD SHAW

Following Sir Ken's presentation in Brighton, his books and talks greatly influenced my own work within education, particularly regarding creativity. Later in my career, he publicly endorsed the innovations at my school, and he became a mentor for an international education project, which my school is involved in. In addition to feeling very well supported by Sir Ken and others like him, in our pursuit of playfulness and imagination, he had another important message, which I feel is integral to the success of our self-development. "Human resources are like natural resources," he said in his speech. "They are often buried deep. You have to go looking for them; they are not just lying around on the surface. You have to create circumstances where they show themselves." This is an empowering message because it invites us to explore the riches of our inner realms and it is also a promise of what lies ahead. Our "natural resources" of imagination, adventure, creativity, and playfulness are within us all. They are like buried treasure, and it is up to us to discover them.

I lost count of the number of derelict houses, spooky old barns, and mysterious forests that I explored with my friends as a child. We didn't want to know what lay ahead of us, and we got a buzz out of discovering new environments, such as hidden valleys and magical gardens. Every weekend we would pack some food and drink (although never enough) and then head for the hills. We would always weave an exciting story into our adventures, which we would convince ourselves was true. It usually involved some sort of intrigue and the possibility of being chased off private land by a farmer or the law. We embraced the moment fully, and although we always returned home feeling hungry and thirsty, our imaginations would have been heartily fed. I remember feeling completely alive during these times and felt like I was somehow larger than life—invincible and free.

Playfulness, adventure, and imagination can help us to explore the world around us. They alleviate anxiety and enhance our feelings of happiness and optimism. They help us to cope with all sorts of challenges and they rekindle our enthusiasm for life. This is why they are so powerful and promote rapid leaps in our self-development.

Carpe Diem—Seize the Day

"The purpose of life is to live it, to taste experience to the utmost, to reach out eagerly and without fear for newer and richer experience."

ELEANOR ROOSEVELT

The week after I climbed the tree in my garden there was another storm. My parents had taken my sister and me to visit our grandmother, so I wasn't at home that day. This time, the storm was even more immense and powerful than the previous one, and on this occasion, a bolt of lightning hit the tree. The lightning split the trunk in two and had caused a fire to start from the inside out. The aftermath was dramatic. When we returned home, we could see that although no other trees or foliage in our garden were damaged, the tree's blackened frame and smoldering branches looked apocalyptic. To my seven-year-old delighted self, this sight was absolutely amazing. What I loved at the time, and still enjoy to this day, is that had I not climbed the tree the previous week and experienced the power and majesty of the storm, I would never have had that opportunity again. My adventure in the tree helped to shape me. I had seized the moment and received its gifts. What I want to do now as an adult is to seize opportunities again, to be playful in the world, and to have adventures. What other gifts lie ahead with this attitude to life only time will tell, but they are there for us all. The spirit of adventure awaits us, and we were born to be wild.

TOP TIPS

1. Grab a notebook, or a piece of paper, and write down your thoughts and insights as we explore the concepts within this book.

2. Today, explore one place that you have never gone to before. It doesn't need to be far away and could be right on your doorstep. It might be a street you have always passed yet never been down previously. Perhaps it is a park or woodland that you have been too busy to visit but really want to see. Or, on your travels out and about, take a different route to your usual one and see where it takes you.

3. Take a picture with your phone of what you see. Save it and build up a bank of "unexplored" places.

4. You are bound to have thoughts like, *I'm too busy for this. I'll do it tomorrow.* If this happens, that is okay. The more we do this, the easier it will become. This simple act of exploring will help you to see things with fresh eyes. It will loosen up your mind and build your natural curiosity about the world around you.

5. Spend some time daydreaming and imagining yourself in places and with people who inspire you. Notice how you feel when you do this. Again, you may have a critical inner voice advising that you don't have enough time to daydream. Don't worry, simply notice the thoughts and feelings you have when they appear, but most importantly, indulge your imagination a bit and enjoy the process.

6. Identify an inspirational and positive character, in fiction or reality, who has inspired you. Perhaps they are a character from your favorite TV show or a book that you quite enjoyed, or, maybe, they are a historical character. Can you imagine having the positive qualities of that person? How do you feel physically and emotionally when you evoke the traits of this character?

7. This is all about rekindling your enthusiasm for life and firing up your imagination again. Like a car that hasn't been started and driven in a while, it might take a while to put our imagination into first gear. This is the point of these simple tips. The main thing is to relax and not to overanalyze your thoughts. Once you have begun this process, it will get easier and more enjoyable.

8. Doodle in your notebook. I will explain this bit in the next few chapters.

2

BREAKING THE RULES

Dead Crows' Island is a mysterious and magical piece of land in the Chiltern Hills, occupying an area of about six acres. I distinctly recall the black, murky water that surrounded it, and the long trek that my childhood friends and I would undergo in order to get there. A river courses through marshy fields and dense woodlands in the lead-up to the island that my friends and I would follow in order to reach it. The length of the journey and the nature of the terrain meant that water would soak through our shoes and make us shiver. Over many years, the river must have silted up and created the natural island, which my friends and I later stamped with its dramatic name.

Once we had reached our destination, it would take a collective effort and ingenuity to cross the water and get to the island. There were countless occasions when we didn't quite make it. The riverbed was heavily silted, so if we fell in, our feet would sink deeply into the cold mud, all the way up to the waist, before anyone could haul us out with a stick or a piece of rope. We would make rafts and build bridges to get there and were always fantastically ill-prepared for every adventure. One time, we managed to lasso a rope around the branch of a tree that hung across the water. The plan, of course, was to swing across the river, which we took turns to do, swinging from one side to the other. Without exception, each one of us swung by the rope and then hung motionless above the water, caught halfway between the island and the mainland, before eventually sliding down the rope and into the cold, boggy water. It was then a case of us having to wade through the water to the other side.

We were so intent on reaching Dead Crows Island because the land itself was both exciting and weirdly horrifying to our childhood minds and imagination. The ground was littered with numerous shotgun cartridges and hanging from the branches of the huge oak trees—the only living things on the island—were the carcasses of hundreds of crows. Their haggard frames were in various states of decomposition. Some were freshly shot, while others were simply skeletal remains. The most gruesome specimens were somewhere halfway between these two states of decay. Black feathers, disembodied wings, battered skulls. We were utterly fascinated. Adding to the drama of Dead Crows Island and the epic task of reaching it was that it was on private property. It didn't take a genius to work out that the owners were in possession of multiple firearms and it was obvious, from the number of dead crows that were blasted across the land, that they were more than happy to use them. This all added to the excitement and adrenaline for our ten-year-old selves. We were breaking the rules and it felt fantastic.

Know the Rules to Break the Rules

"Bend the rules only if you have learned them; break the rules only if you have mastered them."
MATSHONA DHLIWAYO

Later in life, I began to understand the intentional act of rule breaking and the mechanics behind the concept of rules when I was at art school in the 90s. I was living in London and away from home for the first time and was being exposed to various mind-expanding concepts and unusual approaches to life. Part of my training was to learn, in detail, about the master artist Pablo Picasso. He was a fearless genius and expert rule breaker on every level. I remember being deeply impressed and surprised to learn that Picasso's traditional paintings, drawings, and sculptures were of the highest standard, comparable in skill to the Renaissance masters. Although Picasso is most famous for his rule-breaking art form, Cubism, he was also able to paint and draw from life in a conventional and realistic style. And it was because he was highly accomplished in the use of traditional art that Picasso was able to develop completely new and groundbreaking art forms, which, at the time, shaped and rocked the entire art world.

Picasso revealed the secret behind his approach to art in a famous quote, "Learn the rules like a pro, so that you can break them like an artist." He was referring to the formal elements of art, or what others have called the "grammar" of art. If we learn the grammar correctly, we can then play with the rules or break them imaginatively. The same is true for poetry, which often departs from the conventions of the written word. However, a poet must first learn to read and write expertly before they can imaginatively bend the rules.

"Twas brillig, and the slithy toves
Did gyre and gimble in the wabe:
All mimsy were the borogoves,
And the mome raths outgrabe."
JABBERWOCKY, LEWIS CARROLL

Picasso's words are particularly inspiring and liberating for us because they can be applied to the way we live our lives today. If we identify and understand the rules we live by, whether they are our own rules or the rules of a group or institution, we can then decide, in the moment, whether or not they are a true reflection of our current beliefs and intentions. Then, if we wish to, we can break a particular rule.

Although some rules are necessary and helpful, others sometimes stifle our creativity and inhibit the progress of our self-development. It is, therefore, important for us to break a few of them in order to invigorate our creativity and feelings of happiness, and the way to do this is through our imagination. In turn, the more we liberate ourselves from unhelpful and self-imposed rules, the more free-spirited we feel. If we learn the rules like a pro, only then can we break them like artists.

My childhood friends and I knew the rules. We knew that we shouldn't trespass. We knew that we shouldn't trek across the land in our trainers instead of Wellington boots. We knew that swinging on ropes to cross rivers, collecting gun cartridges, and inspecting the corpses of dead animals were all frowned upon. But we still did it! And we broke all of these rules creatively and imaginatively. We weren't hurting anyone or doing any real harm. We were just being free-spirited and a little bit naughty. This playful, light-hearted attitude to life is one that we can adopt as adults and is integral to our journey toward becoming wild and carefree again.

Breaking our own rules is really about enhancing the side of ourselves that exhibits independence of thought and action. To begin with, let's briefly examine the rules we adhere to and identify where they come from:

- Are your rules self-imposed?

- Are they rules of a group or other individual?

- Are they historical or new?

We don't need to dwell too long on this. We can just begin to foster a gentle and growing awareness of what rules we abide by and intuitively feel whether or not they are relevant to our lives today. This is not about replacing old rules with new ones, nor is it about having no rules at all. We are simply being invited to see where our rules come from, and then allow them to evolve, disappear completely, or continue to abide by them. If we become pros and experts about our rules, the rules will serve us well, if and when we need them. This is instead of our rules being our masters, simply because they exist and because we feel that we have to follow them.

Go on, Be a Rebel

"As a rule, I believe people shouldn't follow rules; rules should follow people."

ERIC MICHA'EL LEVENTHAL

Breaking, or updating, our long-held and cherished rules can be challenging. Most of us have been conditioned to think that we must obey authority, follow rules, and conform to whatever it is that we have been told to adhere to. Hence, it might be helpful to invoke our "inner rebel" and "maverick" to help us with this challenge. Rebelling is key to the art of adventure and playfulness. It is what makes these states of consciousness exhilarating and fun. If we can draw on the part of ourselves that is capable of ignoring our long-held traditions and self-imposed rules, breaking them becomes easy. We have all had that moment when we have had enough of a situation and said, "I'm not doing that anymore!" This feeling usually occurs when we have reached the end of our tether with a circumstance, person, or organization. By thinking and acting like a rebel, rebelling against our own limiting beliefs and those of others, we are invited to release unhelpful rules early on. This is without the stress of soldiering on with certain rules, which we know deep down don't work for us anymore.

Children manage to reach the point where they are happy to ditch certain rules and regulations very quickly. They question the relevance of certain expectations placed upon them and then, after weighing up the consequences of following the rules or not, they often follow their own path. My childhood adventures to Dead Crows Island were an example of this. We looked at the emotional and physical rewards we would gain from breaking the rules by trespassing on the island and compared them to the lack of reward that would be gained from staying at home, unchallenged and probably bored. It was an extremely easy decision to make.

Another way to play with the idea of rule breaking is to think about what our "higher purpose" is. In the same way that Picasso learnt the rules of traditional art in order to break them and, therefore, revolutionize the art world, there is a quiet revolution stirring within each of us, too. Our higher purpose and the point of this revolution is our pursuit of happiness, the adventure of a lifetime, the liberation of our creative imagination, and our freedom. If we hold this in mind, before we decide to either follow or break a rule, it can act as a guide before we take any action.

***

Returning to Sir Ken's thought-provoking statement from the previous chapter, "Imagination is the source of every human achievement," we can see that imagination is the driving force behind human development and not the slavish adherence to a set of rules. We can have guiding principles that change and evolve organically, and that serve us, but blindly following rules allows no room for our independence, creative flow, and imagination. As Sir

Ken points out, many of our educational establishments, governments, and other individuals and organizations have historically cautioned us against this philosophy for life. Imagination has been "systematically jeopardized." But just as we all broke a few rules when we were children, in order to discover the world around us, so, too, can we break a few rules in adulthood. Our imagination needs to be unleashed in order for us to achieve our goals and reach our full human potential. We must allow our inner rebel and inner maverick to navigate our way toward our symbolic islands, using imagination as our guide and motivation. We will get wet and muddy along the way, of course. We will fall from rope swings as we attempt to reach our destination, and we will have to be ingenious and creative along our journey. But if we can become more aware and knowledgeable about the rules we abide by, we will be able to decide in the moment whether they are relevant or not. We will become creative artists, leading our personal revolution toward a more carefree and imaginative life. Rules are supposed to be helpful guides, not weighty constraints that stifle us. So, let's travel light— less rules; more freedom.

***

Whenever I returned from Dead Crows Island and other adventures, occasionally my dad would tell me off for either being too late or getting my clothes covered in mud. He wasn't a tyrannical father in the least, but he did perform the role of all good parents and give me some guidance on how to behave. After all, it wasn't me who had to wash my dirty clothes and it wasn't me worrying where my son had gone. Accordingly, depending on the offence, he would sometimes sanction me. Last year, before he died, my dad told me that he always admired my minor rule breaking as a child and was very proud of my maverickism in adult life: "You're a chip off the old block. I've always loved breaking the rules myself!" I don't feel that there is any contradiction between my dad's historical actions when he cautioned me and his recent words of support. Parents are meant to guide their children. However, it is also very natural to break a few rules and for the rules to evolve and change according to circumstances, timing, and other factors. This is where the act of breaking the rules in support of our creativity and imagination becomes a subtle art form. The more we practice the act of rebellion, the more skilled we become. And the more skilled we become, the greater the rewards.

No Rule Is Set in Stone, Especially Your Own

*"Sometimes we have to step out of our comfort
zones. We have to break the rules.
And we have to discover the sensuality of fear.
We need to face it, challenge it, dance with it."*

KYRA DAVIS

We know that rules are extremely necessary in certain circumstances. They can help to shape us and guide us. As a headmaster, I administer plenty of sanctions to my pupils for rule breaking—ranging from a cautionary word to detentions at lunchtime. Without any rules at all, my school would be chaotic and unsafe for everyone. However, I am always open to negotiation and willing to see things from a child's perspective.

A few weeks ago, an 11-year-old pupil was sent to my office for accessing a part of the school that was out of bounds. He was due to receive a detention because in the absence of any adult supervision, we were unable to ensure the boy's safety in the area he had intentionally and knowingly accessed. It is not that we discourage adventure and exploration at the school. That would be rather ironic!

We actually embrace adventure and freedom and have an area of 120 acres of farmland, including two large lakes, attached to the school within which the children can experience a great deal of freedom. On this land, which we call "The Marsh," we encourage children to explore, fish, light fires, and engage in the natural world. The children sail boats, shoot rifles, skin rabbits, and pluck pigeons. It is an unconventional and outward-looking approach to education. However, with other people's children, we have a moral duty to ensure that we can see them while they explore the land, in case they run into any difficulty. In addition to keeping an eye on them ourselves, we empower our children to make decisions for themselves; for example, we teach them that reeds are a sign of deep water. They therefore know that if they walk into the reeds, they are likely to get wet.

The rules at the school are for the safety of the children, but they are not set in stone. I questioned the child who was sent to me for being out of bounds and asked him why he did this. His response was so excellent that I let him off his detention. He said, "A person who never made a mistake never tried anything new." He then added, "Albert Einstein said that!" There was nothing precocious in the way that he said this to me; he was completely genuine and very respectful. How could I punish a child after he had said that? We agreed that he wouldn't access that area of the school again, at least not without an adult, and then had an amazing philosophical conversation about his response. No sanction was necessary.

Learn the rules like a pro and break them like an artist. I think that this boy was the perfect example of Picasso's words. Children do this very naturally and so can we. Rule breaking is a necessary and natural process, which is both enjoyable and powerful in our pursuit of happiness and freedom. Becoming a "Wild Thing" includes us becoming more aware of our perceived constraints and then creatively and imaginatively letting them go—with our higher purpose in our minds and hearts. Of course, we will rattle a few people's cages along the way, but that is better than us living in a cage of our own making.

TOP TIPS

1. Think about the rules you adhere to in your life today. Which rules have you never really resonated with and which ones would you love to get rid of if you could? Make a note of these.

2. If you could break a rule right now, what would it be? Indulge your imagination and see yourself breaking it. What happens in your scenario? How does it make you feel?

3. Now imagine breaking a different rule and visualize the outcome being really positive. Feel as if your maverickism and rebellion has paid off. You feel exhilarated. You feel strong. People around you feel inspired to embrace their own freedom and to follow your example.

4. Break a small rule today. What happens? Record your experience.

5. If the rules and constraints in your life were not there, what would you be doing right now? What small steps could you take today toward living the life of your dreams without these chains around you?

6. Any negative thoughts and doubts should be acknowledged but not dwelled upon when following these tips. Focus on positive thoughts and allow yourself to enjoy the process.

3

STEPPING INTO THE MAGIC

Have you ever noticed how children seem to be able to experience heightened levels of happiness? They appear to access these euphoric states of consciousness on a daily basis. Just look at a school full of children as they spill out of their classrooms and onto the playground for break time. I have been witnessing this for years at my school, and the same thing happens every time. All of the children run outside, squealing with delight and joy, and continue running around, smiling and laughing, until break time has finished. The children appear to be ecstatic and elated. They are fully engaged and absorbed in their games and appear to be fully present in the moment. Children are totally and intensely active while they play. They also see the world around them with completely fresh eyes and are excited by new experiences. For many of them, they are seeing and experiencing some things for the very first time. The newness of everything helps children to stay present and gives them an acute sense of awe and wonder about their lives. It is this combination of physical activity and children's ability to stay in the present that enables them to access feelings of happiness regularly. This happiness easily transforms into flow, euphoria, and ecstasy for children.

Ecstasy and Elation

"Occasionally in life, there are those moments of unutterable fulfillment which cannot be completely explained by those symbols called words.
Their meanings can only be articulated by the inaudible language of the heart."
MARTIN LUTHER KING JR.

We can experience heightened states of happiness in numerous, often surprising, ways. I recently experienced something, which felt euphoric, while riding my bicycle to work. It didn't require me to do anything special, other than for me to be on my bike at a particular time and place. I ride my bike to and from school and travel about 100 miles a week. The thought of this felt like an impossible task before I actually did it! The journey is roughly ten miles each way, and the route passes through some truly stunning countryside. I am not racing at top speed while I ride, so the experience, combined with the inspiring scenery, is extremely enjoyable. Also, the more I ride, the fitter I get; so, the task has become easier over time. Part of the trip includes passing through a few miles of low-lying marshland, which I cycle through at about 7 a.m. The temperature drops considerably on the lowland and the road is completely flat and smooth, so I usually keep up a steady pace at this time. When I have traveled in my car, I have hurtled along with the radio on and with my head full of various thoughts. On reflection, I feel that I have been quite detached from my surroundings while traveling by car. Riding a bike is much slower, of course, and one is fully exposed to the elements without being screened off from the world by metal and glass. Because of this, I have been noticing how truly beautiful the landscape is around me. I take in the different aromas from the trees and the fields and notice the changing colors of the seasons.

On this occasion, the sun was rising above the sea and was casting its light across the marshland. The clouds were a kaleidoscopic spectacle of indigo, amber, and pink and appeared as if they had been sculpted out of some sort of cosmic material. The beauty was truly breathtaking! The deep, golden light of the sun drenched huge swathes of the land around me and created a psychedelic, almost mind-altering, scene. One of the fields to my right was packed full of quite fat-looking sheep. These were all vividly lit up by the sun and appeared bright golden in color. By contrast, the sheep, which were still in the shadow of the hedgerows, appeared to be blue and made me shiver to look at them. The hawthorn bushes and rowan trees either side of me were intricately lit by the sun, and the autumn colors looked like clusters of galaxies in their variety and magnificence.

I can honestly say that I felt elated by the beauty of it all. I felt connected to everything and somehow occupying a timeless state of consciousness. If I had left for work in my car, I would have missed all of this completely. The day before and the day after this event, the sky was dark and overcast, so this felt quite unique and magical. I also reflected on how my feelings were similar to those I sometimes have when I am on holiday and watch a beautiful sunset. We have all sipped wine on a beach somewhere, chatting about how our lives could be more enjoyable if we spent more time feeling calm and present, soaking in the natural beauty around us. It always feels slightly unattainable and somewhat like wishful thinking at the time and can make us feel nostalgic about the experience before it has even finished. Here, out on the marshes, it felt like I was on holiday. I felt complete freedom, deep happiness, and totally inspired. It was a state of ecstasy that made me smile and laugh. The experience felt euphoric and otherworldly. At that moment I felt complete.

States of ecstasy and flow, feeling invincible, existing beyond time, and feeling that we can achieve anything are real states of consciousness accessible to everyone. Children occupy these heightened states of happiness regularly; most experience them on a daily basis. As I did on the morning of my bike ride, adults can access these euphoric states, too. And it is surprisingly easy to achieve once we understand the mechanics and the science of happiness.

When I have visitors to my school, I like to give them a spin on the back of the school quad bike. It is a beast of a machine, which rips across the land effortlessly and at great speed. It is like being on my bicycle, but much louder, faster, and a lot more dangerous. It is a winner with all of our guests and feels like I am taking them on a crazy fairground ride! I will take them around the entire 120 acres of our land and show them our lakes and other features of the habitat.

Because we run a farm on the marsh, we have a small herd of sheep, which we periodically send to market, and a herd of six Asian water buffaloes, which are permanent residents on our marsh. Invariably, the water buffaloes will chase the quad bike as we hurtle across the fields. If we are lucky, we occasionally come across a flock of swans on one of the lakes. Scores of majestic-looking birds will lift off and take flight together. It is an amazing sight!

After the experience on the quad bike, visitors often report feelings of exhilaration and elation. A frequent comment from visitors is that they wish that they were children again and could attend the school. They feel excited, passionate, and full of life. Visitors also spend a lot of time with the children around the fire, making things, cooking, whittling sticks, and taking part in the other ongoing activities. Essentially, we encourage our adult visitors to play. Being outside, seeing the water buffaloes, inspecting the beehives, and racing around on the quad bike inspire feelings of euphoria and flow in our guests every time. I love giving people these enjoyable experiences and receiving their feedback. When children and adults express this level of joy, I call it "stepping into the magic" because the sensations have "magical" qualities such as timelessness, inspiration, and flow.

The Flow

"Aim for the moon. If you miss, you may hit a star."
WILLIAM CLEMENT STONE

The renowned Hungarian-American psychologist Mihaly Csikszentmihalyi has conducted considerable research into our understanding of happiness and identified the heightened state of consciousness, which we now call "flow." The flow occurs when we are completely immersed in an activity and feel totally engaged and fulfilled. This is how I felt during my recent bike ride and how my visitors often feel after their tour of the marsh. Flow also helps to explain the heightened states of happiness exhibited by children while they play.

In his 2016 TED talk on the subject titled "Flow—the secret to happiness," Csikszentmihalyi explains, "There's this focus that, once it becomes intense, leads to a sense of ecstasy, a sense of clarity: you know exactly what you want to do from one moment to the other . . . sense of time disappears, you forget yourself, you feel part of something larger."

In his book on the subject, Csikszentmihalyi further explains that we are happiest when we are completely absorbed in the task at hand. These are the times when we feel that nothing else seems to matter. We may have other concerns, but they just drift away and seem irrelevant in comparison to our immediate experience. This is the state of flow.

Csikszentmihalyi describes various elements for achieving this state of consciousness. He suggests that we need to have an equal balance of challenge and skill during an activity. This means having a balance between the challenge of our task and our skill while performing it. He says that we must feel in control and yet be challenged by an experience; this often happens during physical exercise. It involves us intentionally engaging in an activity while also pushing ourselves beyond our usual state of being.

Do What Inspires You

"Everything you can imagine is real."
PABLO PICASSO

With this in mind, we are invited to examine which activity or subject matter we would like to experience. Athletes will experience flow during their sporting activities. Artists will experience flow while making their art. Musicians will experience flow while playing music and ramblers while trekking across the countryside. Our choice of activities and subject matters are limitless. We can experience heightened states of happiness and flow while doing anything that inspires us. Therefore, it is important for us to identify what we feel most passionate about . . . what sets our heart alight? What inspires us? If we are enthusiastic about an activity, states of flow and happiness are much easier to attain. This is why children will feel heightened states of happiness while playing the games they enjoy and adventuring to places that inspire them. Again, imagination is the magic key for all of us here. It is only our imagination and creativity that will inspire us to do things in the outside world and take us on a path to try new things. And it is imagination that we must draw upon in order to access these higher states of happiness. We therefore mustn't be afraid to dream, to wish, and to let our imagination explore.

Christopher Bergland, an American professional triathlete, takes the concept of flow to another level with his concept of "superfluidity." He read Csikszentmihalyi's book about flow and realized that he felt this flow when he was running, cycling, and swimming. He learnt that by matching his skill level with the level of challenge he wants to reach, he would lose himself in amazing feelings of euphoria.

By harnessing what he learnt about flow, he went on to break world records in his sport. However, Bergland also found that there were higher tiers to the flow experience. To help him understand these additional levels, he first went on to research the concept of ecstasy. The word ecstasy, which comes from the Greek language, means "to stand outside oneself." It describes the feeling we have when we are fully absorbed and engaged in an activity. Everything feels quite magical during these experiences and we can have feelings of timelessness. Bergland felt like he was experiencing states of ecstasy during his heightened states of flow, which occurred during his sporting activities.

It was when Bergland watched a BBC documentary about quantum physics that he had a eureka moment about these expanded states of happiness and flow. The program described the physical process called "superfluidity." This is where helium, when cooled down, can climb the walls of a container and drip through the bottom of a solid glass. It also appears to swirl infinitely as it cools and flows in every direction, as if it defies the laws of physics. This process, which reflected Bergland's increasing understanding about how our brains work, became an analogy for him to explain what happens in the brain when we experience the kinds of heightened states he felt while performing his sport.

Children access these states of flow and superfluidity regularly and effortlessly. They haven't read the works of Csikszentmihalyi and Bergland or worked out the psychology behind their natural states of consciousness. Children just play and feel ecstatic. This is because they naturally engage with the world in new ways, they freely move their bodies within the physical world, and they embrace their creativity and imagination without a modicum of doubt. By fully engaging in the moment, children are less concerned with the past and not so worried about the future as adults can often be. They are also less self-conscious and happier to simply be themselves. All of these components contribute to their heightened states of happiness.

***

A simple act like riding my bike to work allowed me to access the state of flow and have an ecstatic experience. This is the same way that children engage with the world in an open-hearted and open-minded way. If we remember to slightly raise the challenge level of our experience and match it with our skill level, we will not only experience flow, but also higher states of happiness. Those who intentionally access these states of consciousness report that they have greater creativity, they have "eureka" moments, they have better mental and physical health, and they have more positive experiences in their lives in general.

When I saw the dazzling cloud formations and wild colors on my bike ride, I realized that I could feel this way whenever I choose. Opportunities to step into these magical realms are constant and everywhere. Like a child who plays and explores, we, too, are invited to embrace the adventure and playfulness of our own lives and to reap its many rewards. There is a science behind these ideas and psychologists can begin to explain the mechanics behind them, but nothing compares to us experiencing this way of living for ourselves. The human experience of enjoying life intensely is accessible to us all. The trick is to allow ourselves to experience it.

The field of positive psychology, which Csikszentmihalyi and Bergland belong to, is a constantly evolving science, and several psychologists will freely admit that they do not have all of the answers about the root and the path to happiness. Their theories and findings evolve organically as new research is undertaken and as fresh insights are revealed. Nonetheless, it can be helpful for the rational and logical side of our mind, which is often skeptical about new concepts, to have scientific research to back up these theories. If we need convincing any further and wish to delve deeper into the science of happiness, there are numerous excellent books on the subject of positive psychology. However, all of the research in the world means nothing without action on our part. Usually, we are waiting for the "right moment" before we embark on new adventures and change our outlook and approach to life. We often hold ourselves back from progressing and developing out of fear that we are not ready for the change.

Csikszentmihalyi writes in his book *Flow: The Psychology of Optimal Experience*, "Repression is not the way to virtue. When people restrain themselves out of fear, their lives are by necessity diminished. Only through freely chosen discipline can life be enjoyed and still kept within the bounds of reason."

Drawing again on our inner rebel and inner maverick can help with this. Unlike children, who play and partake in adventure quite naturally and, therefore, access these heightened states of happiness. Adults, on the other hand, sometimes need a bit more encouragement. The maverick within us can give us the courage to give it a go without worrying too much about the end result. Whatever our passion is, whatever switches us on and lights our fire, we should embrace it with open arms.

Let us allow our imagination to discover these powerful and positive states of consciousness. Understanding a little more about the mechanics of our happiness, flow, and euphoric states will mean that we can access these feelings more intentionally and easily. But in the end, only we can decide when to step into the magic of our lives. By identifying what inspires us, we can enjoy being more playful and adventurous yet again. Like children across the globe, stepping into the magic will become a deliberate and frequent activity as we live our lives and explore our world.

TOP TIPS

1. What do you like doing the most in your life? What inspires you? It may be one thing or several things. Write them down.

2. Physical activity is integral to your mental and physical health. Children exercise all the time and we call it play. So, the trick is to do something physical that is also enjoyable. Go for a walk. Ride a bike. You can even climb a tree. The objective is to do it *today*.

3. Once engaged in your physical activity, gently push yourself to the point where you feel that you are challenging yourself. Remember, flow is an equal balance of skill and challenge. What feelings do you have during and after this physical activity?

4. Spend a short time (begin with five minutes and build from there) using your senses to experience the present

moment. What can you see? What can you hear? What other sensations do you have? This is about being in the moment, so try to ignore thoughts about the past and the future. This will be difficult to begin with, but don't worry. Allow your thoughts to come and go. The more you practice, the better you will get at this. While focusing on the moment, deepen your breath. This will help you to relax and to be in the here and now.

5. Immediately after you have tuned into the present moment, engage in an activity that you enjoy and love—one that really inspires you. Your brain will make the connection between you being in the present moment and enjoying your life. This, in turn, will help you to enjoy your activity more and encourage you to be in the moment more frequently as well.

6. Doodle some more!

4

FINDING BURIED TREASURE

Children adore nature. They are fascinated by the richness and diversity of the animal kingdom, from sea creatures to the animals that live on land. What child hasn't marveled at the miracle of birds in flight, or the numerous creepy crawlies of the insect world? Plants, too, offer a special kind of excitement, especially when children are in direct contact with them. They ignite enquiry and the desire to explore and discover. Most children will climb trees, explore dense undergrowth, and wonder at exotic flowers if given the opportunity to do so. Despite the decline in most children's exposure to nature, their interest in the natural world has rarely diminished over the years.

Children and young people's commitment to activism, in order to protect the environment, is testimony to their connection to it. The climate change rallies, organized by young people, have shown that they care passionately about nature. They will go as far as to flout the laws and conventions of the land in order to make their point and to show their allegiance to the natural world.

But how often do they actually spend time in nature? Recent studies suggest that, for many, as little as 5 percent of a child's life is spent outside.

At my school, we enable the children to have regular and frequent access to nature through the use of the marshland attached to our main school site. Out on the marsh, regardless of the weather, the children discover and explore raw nature in all its majesty.

The marsh is the seasonal habitat for numerous migrating waterbirds, which fly to the region from as far afield as Russia and the African continent. Many of the rare species of fauna and flora on the site have an unbroken lineage stretching back to prehistoric times. These facts alone fire the imagination, making the marsh feel like it is a portal to a lost world.

The children also come into direct contact with the school's honeybees as well as our water buffaloes, chickens, sheep, ducks, and goats. We recently introduced an array of reptiles to the marsh, including hundreds of common lizards and snakes—all indigenous to the region—which have added to the awe, wonder, and magic of the land. The children, of course, are thrilled by it all.

***

Every Sunday evening, back in my childhood, my family and I would watch natural history programs, presented by the renowned naturalist Sir David Attenborough. I remember feeling completely inspired by the remote locations he would visit and the exotic animals he would show the viewers.

Sir David has continued to inspire me during my adulthood. Now in his 90s, he champions the environment and warns the world's governments about the dire consequences of ignoring the fact that nature and human life are inseparable.

In a similar way that the climate change protests have led to a discussion about the environment, Sir David

Attenborough's campaigning and lobbying have shone a spotlight on the modern world's disconnection with nature.

However, watching TV debates and occupying the streets in towns and cities, in my view, must be accompanied by each of us spending real time in nature, especially if we are to reconnect with the natural world authentically and deeply. Without a genuine emotional connection to nature, there is no incentive to protect it.

When I was a boy, on the weekends, my friends and I would explore the woodlands, farmland, and hills where we lived and immerse ourselves in these environments from dawn until dusk. We got muddy, sunburnt, or chilled to the bone, depending on the season. Always on some sort of adventure, we would inevitably encounter some new animal, find hidden environments, and trek for miles and miles as we tried to find our way back home from each far-flung location. The positive impact this lifestyle had on our minds, bodies, and spirits cannot be overstated. It was the blueprint for the years to come.

However, mentioning a lack of exposure to nature is not simply about feeling nostalgic about a golden age in childhood. Nor is it something that people would like to engage with more often simply for the sake of it. Spending time in nature has numerous benefits, which are hugely positive physically, emotionally, and mentally to both children and adults alike.

The benefits, for adults, can be enhanced when we engage with the natural world in the playful spirit of a child. This means adopting a lightness and a sense of curiosity about nature and fostering a sense of awe and wonder. This playful mindset will result in us feeling deeply inspired and uplifted and lead us to reconnect further with the natural world. Ultimately, it will result in us experiencing a deeper connection with ourselves and with those around us.

Nature in Our Imagination

"Just living is not enough . . .
one must have sunshine, freedom, and a little flower."
HANS CHRISTIAN ANDERSEN

In case you are now thinking, *I haven't got time to hang out in nature* or *I would love to connect with nature more, but I live in a town*, you don't need to rush off to the hills just yet. For now, just kick back and let us connect with nature using our imagination. Make yourself comfortable, relax, and take a few deep breaths.

Now, imagine yourself in a beautiful and inspiring natural landscape. It could be an ancient forest with huge, leafy oak trees rising out of the lush, green undergrowth. The aroma of woodland flowers, moss, and earth pervade the scene.

Perhaps, instead, you are on top of a mountain, with peaks and valleys as far as the eye can see. From here, you look out to the misty blue horizon and feel the smooth granite rock beneath your bare feet. Or maybe you are on a sandy beach, listening to the ebb and flow of the waves. Feeling the warm sun on your body, you sink into a deeply relaxed state of consciousness. You feel at peace. You feel complete.

Try to use all of your senses to evoke the scene in your imagination. What can you see, hear, smell, touch, and taste?

Imagine that you are happily on your own and that you feel at ease and uplifted by the feelings of tranquility and freedom that the environments offer you. And if you wish to change your imaginary environment in any way, or fancy occupying a completely different one, then feel free to do so.

While enjoying the experience of these real or imagined places, become aware of your breath. Breathe in deeply through your nose and exhale through your mouth. And with each exhalation, feel the tension in your face, neck, and shoulders slip away.

Soften your eyes and allow this relaxed feeling to flow throughout your body, from your arms to your hands, and from your legs to your feet.

Do not push this process. Just allow the relaxed feeling to come at its own pace. Within these imagined worlds, time is infinite and there is no rush to do anything. You are completely safe and free. The effect on your minds and emotions, while imagining beautiful natural places, can be positive and immediate and to a great extent. Notice how you feel as you immerse yourself in these environments.

What sensations can you feel in your body?

How do you feel emotionally?

And when you are ready, try to sustain the feeling of well-being and calm as you leave these imagined realms.

We can access these environments easily and reap the emotional rewards whenever we wish. Allowing time for our imaginations to take us to beautiful natural spaces can also inspire us to make time to visit natural environments within the physical world.

The Natural World

"You must live in the present, launch yourself on every wave, find your eternity in each moment."
HENRY DAVID THOREAU

There are multiple benefits to spending time in the real world of nature, which have been extensively researched and documented. Being in any natural environment, whether it be by a river or lake, walking in the woods, or sitting on a beach, can inspire feelings of happiness and can even alleviate depression and anxiety. Studies have shown how spending time in nature can eliminate fatigue and lower one's blood pressure. The great outdoors can improve our self-esteem, increase our creativity, and boost our immune system. The health benefits to mind and body are profound and far-reaching.

The positive effect of a single exposure to nature, such as a walk in a park, tending your garden, or walking through a wooded area on the way to work, can last for as much as seven hours after the person has had the experience, according to studies.

This response was recorded in a study developed in 2018 by Dr. Andrea Mechelli of King's College London. Dr. Mechelli asked a number of people to use an app on their phone called "Urban Mind." The app tracked the movements of the people in the study throughout their day. This included times when they would have some sort of contact with nature such as walking through a park. The participants were then asked various questions about where they were, what they were doing, and how they felt at the time.

The urban settings, where the study took place, were full of roads and buildings with occasional natural features, like parks and trees. Yet, without exception, everyone involved in the study reported feelings of sustained happiness after even the smallest contact with nature.

Interestingly, not everyone had the same reaction after exposure to nature. People with a greater risk of developing mental health problems, such as depression and anxiety, had a greater positive response to nature than any other group. For me, this is very telling, indicating that nature is an extremely powerful healer.

This is all very well, but what about the lack of time we often seem to have in our lives? We are always doing something more urgent and important than connecting with nature. We usually feel that this kind of thing can wait until the future, when we are less busy.

Children are great at living in the present moment. Generally speaking, they spend less time reliving the past and worrying about the future than adults do. From the moment my twin daughters were able to crawl and explore their surroundings, I noticed that they were fascinated by the natural world. Now, at the age of three, whether they are picking up stones to see what lies beneath them, or watching the birds and butterflies in our garden, the girls are completely immersed in the present moment while playing outside.

Because of the twins' insatiable appetite for being outdoors, coupled with the need for an adult to keep a watchful eye on them, my wife and I have found ourselves seeing the world through the eyes of a child again. Crawling through bushes, seeing what is living in the undergrowth, gazing at the sky, and marveling at plants and animals have become frequent activities that we share with our children.

Lying on the ground and carefully examining an ant, as it navigates its way across tiny stones and in and out of miniature holes, is not something that I would usually take time to do. However, my girls inspire me to get down on their physical level and to look at things in a completely different and more playful way.

Just a few seconds of truly being present and observing nature with the awe and wonder of a child can inspire sensations of calm and relaxation and expand our mind in unexpected ways.

Tuning in to the feeling of well-being, which we can attain when visualizing natural spaces or when we are in physical nature, has a timeless quality, similar to that which we experience during the state of flow.

Time, or lack of it, is quite often the excuse we give ourselves for not venturing into the great outdoors. We dream of climbing mountains and swimming in freshwater pools. We imagine ourselves soaking up the sun on exotic beaches and going on long walks in beautiful forests. But these things are for tomorrow, next week, or next year. Perhaps when we retire. The reality is that time is an illusion.

The strange irony about time is that when we make time to go out into nature, or to visualize, we don't lose precious moments. Instead, time appears to stretch, our minds become clearer, and problem-solving and feeling positive and free become almost effortless.

We are conditioned from an early age to become chained to the clock and to constantly believe that we have little time and must wait until tomorrow to enjoy the good things in life. This leads to us missing the magic of our lives. Although it may, at first, feel awkward and unnatural, "making time" to do the things that we enjoy, and particularly making time to immerse ourselves in nature, is essential to our overall well-being. If we can get through the first few moments of feeling like we ought to be doing something else, spending time in the natural world will clear our minds and ignite our enthusiasm for life. Surely that is what life should be about, isn't it?

The Art of Getting Lost

"Learn to enjoy every minute of your life. Be happy now.
Don't wait for something outside of yourself
to make you happy in the future.
Think how really precious is the time you have to
spend, whether it's at work or with your family.
Every minute should be enjoyed and savored."

Earl Nightingale

By engaging with the natural world in a playful and inquisitive way, we will experience increased happiness and improve our physical and mental health. This, in turn, will help us to cope with life's challenges more effectively because health and happiness underpin our ability to solve problems.

Integral to this concept is the message that we can access this magical realm in our local park, back garden, or by simply stepping out of our front door. Nature is everywhere, and the spirit of adventure is easily accessible, anytime, anywhere.

We can take this a step further by tapping into our inner child, and instead of only experiencing familiar places deciding to venture onto uncharted paths. This is when we actively look for hidden places and go on the hunt for "buried treasure."

When did we last explore a woodland, county lane, or an open field, simply for the sheer fun of exploring it?

It doesn't matter if we can't remember. We can do it today. We might even get lucky and discover that we are lost!

There is an art to getting lost. During the times when we venture off the beaten track or do something completely new, we sometimes lose our bearings. This is because our senses are heightened and everything feels fresh and undiscovered; we stay in the moment and lose track of time. At these times, we may forget the way back to the start of our journey.

If we stay in the moment and embrace this feeling of being lost for a while, something remarkably interesting takes place. Whether it is the time on the clock that we have no idea about or the location of our physical whereabouts, in that moment, it is possible to find real treasure.

It may be a new environment that inspires us . . . trees and plants that we have never seen before. Perhaps it is a feeling of liberation as we immerse ourselves in the freedom of not knowing exactly where we are. Or maybe we have a flash of inspiration as we find ourselves in an unfamiliar environment with our senses heightened. We feel alert and alive.

I have observed children at play in nature and witnessed on countless occasions how they lose themselves in the moment, discover something new, and then lose their bearings. Eventually, they work out where they are and trace their steps back. However, they are quite quick to venture off again. Why? Because the buzz of being in the moment and discovering something new is where the treasure lies. If we marry this concept with being outside in nature, we ignite a magic that children experience frequently, the magic that we lose as we enter adulthood.

At these times we truly become wild things. Our inner treasures, which may have laid buried for years, are revealed again. A magic for us to play with and to explore.

TOP TIPS

1. Visualize beautiful settings in nature. Use all of your senses to conjure the scene and notice how this makes you feel. If a particular setting makes you feel good, return to it often.

2. Harness the feeling of well-being that you feel while visualizing. Try to continue the sensation of calm and completeness after the experience.

3. Get out in nature. Whether it be a single oak tree on the roadside, a park in the town, a beach, or a woodland. You deserve to connect with the natural world and to reap its many benefits to soothe your mind, body, and spirit.

4. Remember that time is an illusion. Become its master, not its slave.

5. Try getting lost. When you are lost, hold your nerve. Embrace the feeling and find the magic within it. Buried treasure is always there for you to discover.

6. Study a small insect, like an ant or spider, within its habitat. Get up close and really look. Notice how you feel when you turn your attention back to the larger world.

7. Doodle in your book.

5

BUILDING GRIT AND RESILIENCE

Grit: Courage and determination despite difficulty.
Resilience: The quality of being able to return quickly
to a previous good condition after problems.

CAMBRIDGE ENGLISH DICTIONARY

The small boat, dented and scuffed from years of being hauled in and out of the water, drifted downriver, with five of us on board. It had mismatched oars and fraying ropes, which trailed from the stern. We lay back against its sides, limbs intertwined, gazing at the stars. The river was so still that the night sky was mirrored perfectly in the water. Yet, despite the stillness, a deep and constant undercurrent, undetectable from the surface, pulled us gently along and toward the sea.

I would go down to the river every night with my sons, who were 6 and 13 years old at the time. We would board the little boat with my friends Pete and Mel. They owned the farm through which this magical river meandered. We would begin each night in a caravan on the water's edge, share a bottle of wine, and then launch the boat. Around midnight, we would swim in the water, the reflected stars scattering around our bodies as we laughed and played.

I still don't know exactly how we started going down to the farm. I didn't know Pete and Mel that well before this time, and the river, although only a few minutes from my home, was hidden from the road and difficult to access. There was something about the stark chill of the water when we dived into it, the ramshackle honesty of the sprawling cattle farm, and the unconditional love of my friends that drew me.

Three weeks before our first visit to the farm, my wife and mother of my two sons had died very suddenly from a brain tumor. She had been experiencing headaches for some time, explored various remedies without success, until, reluctantly, she went to the doctor for help. She was shortly diagnosed with incurable cancer and died just six weeks later in our bedroom at home.

The river and my friends became my sons' and my sanctuary—a place where we could just be ourselves. It felt emotionally raw, but it also felt playful. There was a gentleness to the experience, and yet being there demanded strength. It made us surrender to the indescribable process of death, and it forged a resilience within us. And over time, the river, and our connection with one another, would make us ready for the world again.

On this particular occasion, a few weeks into the nightly ritual of us entering the water, I experienced a major shift in consciousness . . . the beginning of my road to recovery.

I dived under the surface and into the cold blackness. As I arched around and back up to the top, I could see the stars darting and shimmering through the water above me. It was freezing cold, forcing me to be completely in the moment.

And for the first time in weeks, when I came up for air, I found myself laughing.

Moving Out of Our Comfort Zones

*"Master yourself, and become king
of the world around you.
Let no odds, chastisement, exile, doubt, fear, or ANY
mental virii prevent you from accomplishing your dreams.
Never be a victim of life; be its conqueror."*

MIKE NORTON

The experience of visiting my friends on their farm and swimming in the river every night laid the foundations for some of my later work in education. Making myself jump into the cold water, experiencing the initial discomfort, and then pushing through with the experience involved me moving out of my comfort zone.

One of the things that I absolutely love about having the marshland at my school is that I have the opportunity to work out on the land. I recently drove the school's quad bike to the far side of the marsh, to where we teach our pupils outdoor learning skills, fishing, and beekeeping. It was raining hard and the ground was heavily waterlogged. A group of about 15 pupils, aged 9, were lighting fires, gathering wood, and erecting shelters with sticks and tarps. The wind was gusting, which meant that the children had to brace themselves against it as they labored to put up makeshift windbreaks.

I joined a small group by one of the fires they had made and sat down for a hot drink and a chat. Despite being wet and cold, all of the children, most of whom were girls, were smiling, happy and getting on with the job at hand. They appeared completely unfazed by the adverse weather conditions and seemed to be relishing the challenge and the opportunity to have moved out of their comfort zones.

The concept of a person having a "comfort zone" was first conceived by psychologists Robert M. Yerkes and John Dodson more than 100 years ago. After many experiments, they concluded that "a state of relative comfort created a steady level of performance." This state of relative comfort was coined the "comfort zone."

However, if an individual desires to increase their performance and develop as a person, they, at times, need to step into a state of "relative anxiety," where their stress levels are slightly higher than normal. The psychologists labeled this state "optimal anxiety," which lies just beyond a person's comfort zone.

So, simply put, Yerkes' and Dodson's research showed that when we move out of our comfort zones, we can make rapid leaps in our personal development.

In light of this concept, the curriculum at my school includes regular opportunities for the children to move out of their comfort zones. Experiences such as working outside in sub-zero temperatures and in the driving rain enable them to do this. Pushing themselves beyond their own perceived limitations, they find that they have immense inner strength and skills, which they would otherwise not have discovered.

Over the years, we have found that even the most fragile of students, sometimes with a plethora of psychological diagnoses such as autism or attention deficit hyperactivity disorder (ADHD), or anxiety, rise to the challenge when faced with difficulties that they must overcome.

It seems clear to me that it is when we are confronted with various challenges and are forced to get through them that we find the inner resources we need in order to be triumphant.

Most children, in my experience, are incredibly good at moving out of their comfort zones; it is natural for them. From the moment they are born, they are faced with huge challenges—from learning to walk and talk to understanding and navigating their way around the complex, and often contradictory, social nuances of the adult world. Then there is school, where children are presented with fresh challenges on a daily basis. Teachers will tell children to undertake new academic tasks, perform in front of their peers, follow intricate instructions, and do physical exercises in uncomfortable weather conditions. Week after week. Year after year. And generally speaking, children develop and improve their skills as expected of them by the adults in charge. After three hours of hard work in the rain, and completely wet and muddy, the children I had visited on the marsh were still smiling. The long walk across the land and back to school still lay ahead of them, but every child had an aura of achievement and power about them.

The inner resources, which the children discover while undertaking challenging activities, will serve them well throughout their lives, particularly within a world full of change and uncertainty. When they move out of their comfort zones, they move into a place where they can grow and achieve. A place where they can go beyond the constraints of others' and their own limiting beliefs about themselves.

I feel like my experience of regularly moving out of my comfort zone on my friends' farm gave me strength and significantly contributed to building my resilience during that challenging time in my life. Passing that knowledge on to the children at my school has been enormously rewarding . . . a gift borne out of adversity.

Harnessing the Chemicals Within Our Body

"Obstacles, of course, are developmentally necessary: they teach kids strategy, patience, critical thinking, resilience and resourcefulness."

NAOMI WOLF

Building grit and resilience are not just about moving out of our comfort zones. There are chemical processes within our bodies that can be cultivated in order to promote these traits.

Helpful chemicals within our bodies are released when we exercise, have physical contact with other people, and we eat well. These chemicals are oxytocin, dopamine, serotonin, and endorphins, to name a few.

Most children have these chemicals coursing through their bodies in abundance. The reason being that they run around a lot as they play, something that adults would label as "exercise." More often than not, children are also extremely physically demonstrative. This is a trait that, like exercise, tends to be left behind in later life. Additionally, children who are looked after well are usually provided with regular and nutritionally balanced meals. As we know, eating well is positive for us on so many levels, and yet with our busy lives, adults often allow healthy eating to lapse.

Physical touch, exercise, and healthy eating release chemicals that are physically and mentally beneficial to us. They promote the light-hearted and playful outlook on life that children exhibit so effortlessly.

Oxytocin

Oxytocin, sometimes called the "love hormone," is usually triggered in the brain by physical contact with a loved one and has a positive impact on other relationships, including those within our family and at work. It can also be released through massage, yoga, and any harmonious contact with another person. This is what was going on when I was connecting with my friends on the farm. Receiving loving hugs and cuddling my boys on the boat flooded my body with oxytocin in abundance.

Dopamine

Then there is dopamine, which is often called the "motivation molecule." It helps us to achieve our goals and focus. It is essential to cultivating the traits of grit and resilience and creates feelings of euphoria as well. I believe that high dopamine levels within my own body are part of the reason I remain positive about the challenges I face within my job. Anyone can increase their dopamine levels by eating foods such as avocados, bananas, meat and poultry, almonds, and pumpkin seeds, among others. Any kind of exercise, from walking to swimming, can also increase our dopamine levels.

Serotonin

The next helpful chemical to spotlight in our bodies is serotonin. This regulates our mood and is boosted by a healthy diet and exercise. I love spending time outside with my family and with the children at school. I feel this boosts my serotonin levels and helps to facilitate my generally happy mood. I also go to the gym when I can and have a fairly balanced diet. In the adult world, we don't always exercise regularly, and we can easily slip into poor eating habits. Turning this around is scientifically proven to create a more positive attitude, with feelings of happiness and optimism seen within anyone willing to embrace the change. Again, being outside on my friends' farm and diving off the boat to swim in the river would have increased the serotonin levels in my body at a time when this was much-needed.

Endorphins

Endorphins occur naturally within our body. They create a positive feeling in the body and mask pain. They are essential to character-building in relation to grit and resilience. Again, eating well and exercising increase endorphin levels. They are also released when engaging in any activity that a person finds pleasurable. Positive thoughts and affirmations, massage, being in nature, and meditation can all release endorphins. Conscious deep breathing has also been proven to top up endorphins within the body, leading to happy feelings and an overall feeling of well-being. The shock of the cold water on my body as I entered the river would have released endorphins in my body each night when I dived in for a swim.

When confronted with life's challenges, which happens to every one of us, this cocktail of natural chemicals within our bodies can help us to overcome them. It doesn't require a complete overhaul of our lifestyle or habits. Even the smallest tweak, such as walking more often and choosing a nutritious meal over an unhealthy one, can lead to significant increases in our overall feeling of well-being.

Of course, I didn't arrive at the period in my life where I would be dealing with the death of a loved one empty-handed. I had many insights during that time, acquired many new skills, and gained useful character traits, but I also had my background and the existing lessons of a lifetime in my arsenal.

I have been blessed to have been raised by parents who modeled grit and resilience as I was growing up. Both my mother and father lived out their childhoods during World War II. My dad was the son of a World War I veteran who had fought in the trenches at the age of 15. He had pretended to be 18 in order to enlist and found himself on the front line in the Battles of the Somme. My dad wasn't evacuated during the war and instead lived in Manchester throughout this time. He used to tell me stories about his family and him hiding under the kitchen table during air raids, only to discover that half of his street had been bombed out by the morning. My mum, who was evacuated to Canada, had an equally tumultuous time when the ship that her family sailed on was torpedoed by the Germans during their journey.

My parents were both very positive and fun people to be around when I was growing up. However, they had little patience for complaints from their children about how hard life can be. They taught us to pick ourselves up when we fell down, brush ourselves off, and continue with life.

However, I think that the most valuable gift bestowed on me by my parents was their positivity and the fact that they encouraged me to focus on my strengths. A philosophy of life endorsed by the scientific field known as Positive Psychology.

The Power of Positive Psychology

"It's only a thought, and a thought can be changed."
LOUISE HAY

Mental health therapy is largely based on the traditional psychology of the 20th century. This has enabled us to become particularly good at identifying a person's issues, and then, in some cases, labeling them. One example of this is anxiety. I don't think that I have ever heard so many children and adults say that they feel anxious about an aspect of their lives than I have in recent years. Yet, constantly identifying with our anxieties shines a spotlight on them and can actually amplify them and rarely makes them go away.

The field of positive psychology flips this way of dealing with mental health on its head. Positive psychology is a scientific approach to studying human thoughts, feelings, and behavior. It focuses on a person's strengths, rather than their weaknesses, building on good things as opposed to solely focusing on our struggles. It focuses on positive experiences like happiness, joy, inspiration, and love; positive character traits including gratitude, resilience, and kindness; and positive institutions, which involve applying positive principles within entire organizations.

Positive psychologists such as Martin Seligman say that an overemphasis on identifying the negative traits, such as a person's anxiety, can disempower them rather than empower them. It is not that we don't genuinely feel anxious at times, but we do need to recognize that this is a natural part of life and that we still need to get on with living, regardless of this uncomfortable feeling.

As a field, positive psychology spends much of its time thinking about areas like character strengths, optimism, happiness, well-being, confidence, and hope, among others. These areas are studied in order to learn how to help people harness them and to flourish and live their lives to the fullest. For example, Martin Seligman says that people who are optimistic and happy have better performance at work and school, are less depressed, have fewer physical health problems, and have better relationships with other people.

A few years ago, I launched a positive psychology project at my school. Part of this involved my staff identifying six positive character traits that we collectively felt would benefit our pupils and staff. These traits were resilience, love of learning, gratitude, forgiveness, teamwork, and kindness.

We then introduced these concepts to the children and staff at every opportunity through our curriculum, philosophy sessions, assemblies, rewards, and displays. As a staff, we also highlighted these traits within each other and discussed them at meetings.

The impact of this action, on the adults and the children within the school, was quite impactful, with most people reporting positive results within a short amount of time. Simply by shifting our focus away from the negative and on to the positive made the school community feel happier and resulted in us being more productive.

Positive psychology proves that this sort of constructive outlook on life is good for us on so many levels. And when it comes to building grit and resilience, focusing on our strengths, rather than our areas for development, is absolutely essential.

All those years ago, while swimming in the river on my friends' farm, I experienced a profound transformation. Only now, after years of working with children and applying the principles of optimal anxiety, positive psychology, and flow, can I begin to explain exactly what happened to me.

It was a combination of several powerful elements. I was moving out of my comfort zone while making myself swim in the cold, dark water. As I swam, I was being physical while activating the helpful chemicals within my body such as endorphins and serotonin. I was combining my experience with play and discovery, rowing the boat at midnight, and diving into the darkness. And I was embracing the present moment, stimulated by the beauty and majesty of the night sky and the shock to my system as my body entered the water. I was surrounded by loving friends and family with whom I was physically affectionate, thus releasing the chemical dopamine into my body.

As I came up to the surface and took my first breath, I started laughing. All five of us did as we played and splashed about in the water. Laughter, whooping, and shouting filled the night air. I felt alive again. I felt like

I did when I was a child—exploring hidden places and getting wet and muddy on my many adventures.

It was as if a switch had flicked on in my mind and everything became illuminated. Just as I had come up from under the surface of the water to breathe again, I was now emerging from the depths of despair in order to live again.

From that moment, I would begin the process of healing my life through joy and through play. I became stronger and more resilient because of the struggle. Grit and resilience are naturally occurring traits, which are abundant in childhood and can be cultivated in adulthood. By seeking out opportunities to step out of our comfort zones— through exercise, by being physically demonstrative, and by improving aspects of our diet—we can set the right conditions in order to build up our strength.

They are character traits that we all possess, however dormant they may appear at present. Grit and resilience are powerful allies in the face of adversity and can be harnessed to move us toward life's great adventures, bringing us joy and discovery.

My experience on the boat provides an analogy for life. Our individual boats will carry us on life's inevitable journey, regardless of what we do. However, the opportunity for us to dive in and to invigorate our existence is always present. We can stay in the relative comfort and safety of our boat, or we can shake things up a bit and dive into the water. Doing the latter will give us strength, provide us with new adventures, and build grit and resilience within us.

TOP TIPS

1. Choose one activity that you feel takes you out of your comfort zone and make yourself do it. Notice your resistance, your reaction before, during, and after the experience.

2. List your positive character traits. Read the list and feel good about it. Add to the list when you think of more traits.

3. Try to eat at least one healthy meal a day.

4. Exercise, even if it is simply going for a walk.

5. Think of an aspect of your life that you find challenging and look for the positive lessons within it. Repeat this for other areas you find challenging.

6. Cuddle more often.

7. Do something that you love doing every day.

8. Treat yourself to a massage.

9. Doodle in your book.

6

GRATITUDE

"**T**hink of an idea to change the world and put it into action." This is the title of a high school assignment, written on a chalkboard, at the beginning of the 2000 film *Pay It Forward*.

Mr Simonet, the class teacher, turns to face his pupils. "The realm of possibility exists where in each of you?" he asks, scanning the classroom. The pupils are silent. "In here," he whispers enigmatically, pointing toward his head.

The camera pans to one particular child who is sitting at his desk. This pupil is Trevor, a seventh-grade pupil. He appears transfixed by his teacher's words.

The next time the class meets, each pupil is invited to present their idea to the teacher and to the rest of the class.

When it is Trevor's turn, he begins by drawing a simple diagram, representing a formula, on the chalkboard. He then explains what it means to his classmates and how using this formula could change the world.

He calls his plan "Pay It Forward," and it works like this—rather than simply repaying a person when they have done you a favor, Trevor suggests that we do a good deed for three other people instead. He says that we must also ask those three people to do a favor for three further individuals. Paying a favor forward and requesting that the recipient of the favor do the same would eventually branch out exponentially and, in time, change the entire world for the better.

Personally, I love the simplicity of this concept. Trevor is only 12 years old in the film, and yet the heady challenge of coming up with an idea to change the world is one that he fully embraces.

Like real life, the film isn't positive throughout. It gets pretty dark at times, and in some ways, it is a portrait of how our often brutal world tramples over the sensitivities of children. It is how our innate playfulness, enthusiasm for life, and wonder about things get replaced with pessimism, conformity, and fear.

Feeling and Expressing Thanks

*"If you're reading this . . .
Congratulations, you're alive.
If that's not something to smile about,
then I don't know what is."*
CHAD SUGG, *MONSTERS UNDER YOUR HEAD*

If nothing else, where there is life, there is hope. Even when things feel a bit bleak at times, we can still express one thing that we are grateful for. *I feel thankful that I am alive.*

To use an analogy, let's imagine that this one gratitude is a seed; something to be watered and tended, but not expecting it to sprout into a fresh green shoot overnight. There is not much to do other than to have an awareness of this seed and to hold it gently within our being.

It might not feel like it at first, but without this seed, which represents our physical existence, no other gratitude, creative ambition, or success in the world is possible. Life is the most precious thing that we possess. It is true when people say that life is a gift.

When we feel gratitude, we are feeling and expressing thanks and appreciation. In 2007, Robert A. Emmons, PhD, began researching the concept of gratitude within the context of positive psychology. Emmons is now the world's leading scientific expert on the subject. He is a professor of psychology at the University of California, founding editor-in-chief of *The Journal of Positive Psychology*, and author of many books on the topic of gratitude.

Following extensive research, Emmons discovered that expressing gratitude improves our mental and physical well-being and impacts our overall experience of happiness. He also found that these positive effects last for a long time after a person has authentically expressed the things that they are thankful for.

Emmons' research revealed numerous benefits that the simple act of expressing gratitude can have on our lives. Some of them are quite surprising and include:

- Improved feelings of connection during challenging times

- Increased self-esteem

- Greater optimism

- Heightened energy levels

- Strengthened heart

- Stronger immune system

- Decreased blood pressure

- Improved emotional intelligence

- Improved academic intelligence

- Expanded capacity for forgiveness

- Decreased stress levels

- Decreased levels of anxiety and depression

Gratitude stimulates the hypothalamus, the central lower part of the brain that controls body temperature, hunger, and the release of chemicals. Research shows that the more we express gratitude, the greater are the benefits and the longer they last.

A commonly used and effective way to promote a grateful outlook on life is to write down the things that we feel thankful for. It works best if this is done on a daily basis. Research shows that the more we do this, the more grateful we become. Recording what we feel grateful for, in writing, can also help our sense of well-being when we look back at our notes and remind ourselves about the good things in life.

However, even if we start simply by expressing thanks for being alive—after all, this is the most fundamentally important gratitude that we can express—all of the benefits listed previously, plus many more, will begin to appear in our lives.

Wherever we are on our life's journey, expressing gratitude can help us in more ways than one. Being thankful for what we have, rather than focusing on what we lack, is imperative to this process. Scientific research tells us that grateful people are typically happier than those who are not, so this should be enough of a reason for us to give it a go.

We can begin by thinking about what we are thankful for once a day. This might be at the end of the day, perhaps before we go to sleep, or first thing in the morning. Whatever feels good and is manageable. If we begin to prioritize expressing gratitude and recognize the things that we appreciate most in our lives, this will soon feel like a natural process, and we will definitely reap its rewards.

One of the biggest obstacles to making the expression of gratitude part of our daily lives is a lack of self-worth. Many of us are in the habit of noticing the good things about others, but we don't apply the same level of admiration to ourselves. Noticing the good things about our lives is essential if we wish to feel happier.

Let us begin by identifying things about ourselves that we like and admire. This could be a character trait, a past achievement, or some other feature about us that we are happy with. Now, look in a mirror and say these things out loud as a gratitude:

*I am thankful for being committed
to my self-development.*

I am grateful that I enjoy learning new skills.

*I give myself gratitude for being
a good friend to others.*

Over the years, the negative comments and conditioning, which may have eroded our sense of self-worth and gratitude, have often been delivered by a person looking us in the eye. This has reinforced the negative statements and embedded them within our minds.

By giving ourselves positive messages and affirmations in the mirror, while looking into our own eyes, we powerfully reverse the impact of the negative messages and replace them with positive ones. This process helps to heal past experiences, including those that we may have had during childhood.

Gratitude and Play

"It is a happy talent to know how to play."
RALPH WALDO EMERSON

I have observed hundreds of children over the years as they enter an empty playground and then make up imaginative games within seconds of being there. Magical worlds open up for them and new adventures are experienced. The sound of laughter and scenes of children having fun manifest immediately.

Of course, children sometimes fall out with one another, and not every playtime is a success, but for most children, and on most occasions, playtime is something that they enjoy. This is because children actively pursue the things that they love to do. This might be a favorite game, finding certain children to play with, or playing in a preferred location.

Once engaged in a game, connecting with their friends and in the right location, children activate their imaginations. Without imagination, children would not be able to make up games or invent unseen worlds and scenarios, which only they and their friends can see.

Children don't lose this ability to imagine and to create because they grow older. This playful outlook on life diminishes due to the pessimism, fear, and conformity that is passed down to them from the adults around them. Fortunately, as we have learnt, playfulness and the spirit of adventure is never lost forever and can be reclaimed with ease. One only has to look deep within and strive to not lose that innate playfulness and imagination.

By weaving together positive affirmations and expressions of gratitude, we can enhance our imaginations and our playful traits. For example, try saying:

I love to play and to have adventures.

Repeat this statement while looking in the mirror. Really feel the intention behind this upbeat and celebratory message. The same message, with a slightly different angle, might be:

I am a playful person with a spirit of adventure.

Or we could experiment by saying:

I can see the opportunity for creativity in everything.

The more we repeat these affirmations and genuinely feel thankful, the more these traits will become embedded deep within us.

We don't have to wait for life to be perfect before we allow ourselves to feel good. Expressing gratitude can be something that we practice regardless of our current situation. And the act of doing so will lift our spirits as soon as we begin.

Appreciating the Little Things in Life

"Be thankful for what you have;
you'll end up having more.
If you concentrate on what you don't have,
you will never, ever have enough."

Oprah Winfrey

It is easy to put off expressing gratitude if we just wait for big things in life to be grateful for. We can find ourselves waiting for a long time if we do this. Gratitude is about feeling thankful for everything, including the seemingly small things. We might be thankful that the weather is pleasant, or perhaps we have just eaten a delicious meal. Maybe we have had a good day at work, or we are enjoying the pleasurable feeling of getting into bed at the end of a long day.

Appreciate the small things in life in order to benefit from the expression of gratitude. Over time, the regular practice of expressing thanks, for even the smallest of things, will shift our mindset to one of positivity and happiness. In turn, our ability to find solutions to problems, and to cope with life's ups and downs, will improve considerably.

As previously mentioned, this sort of authentic positivity will release helpful chemicals such as serotonin and endorphins within our bodies. The more we practice, the happier we will feel and the easier it will be to express further gratitude.

Increasing Our Luck

*"You are the master of your destiny.
You can influence, direct and control
your own environment.
You can make your life what you want it to be."*
NAPOLEON HILL

Wouldn't it be great if we experienced more luck in our lives so that we could have more to feel grateful for? The good news is that we can.

Richard Wiseman, a psychologist from the University of Hertfordshire and author of *The Luck Factor*, spent a decade researching the notion of lucky and unlucky people. Since time immemorial, people have seen how good and bad luck can radically change a person's life. A moment of bad luck can devastate a person's existence, whereas a stroke of good luck can improve someone's life forever.

Wiseman decided to carry out a scientific investigation in order to find out why some people are lucky, while others are consistently unlucky. Why do some people seem to have all of the lucky breaks and fortuitous encounters leading to happiness and success? And why do other people appear to live a life full of seemingly endless disasters and failure?

Hundreds of men and women took part in the research. They were of all ages and occupations and were either extremely lucky or extremely unlucky in life. Wiseman's research revealed that luck is not the result of random chance, or that people are born either lucky or unlucky. Furthermore, his research showed that luck is not the result of possessing some sort of magical ability to manifest good fortune. Instead, Wiseman discovered that a person's thoughts and behavior are the real cause of good or bad luck.

He concluded that good luck is generated using four principles:

1. A lucky person is skilled at creating and noticing chance opportunities.

2. A lucky person listens to their intuition.

3. A lucky person has positive expectations—they are optimistic.

4. A lucky person transforms bad luck into good luck within their minds and in their lives as well. This makes them more resilient.

In one experiment, Wiseman gave lucky and unlucky people a newspaper. He asked them to look through the newspaper and count how many photographs were inside. On the second page, in gigantic letters, were the words: "Stop counting—There are 43 photographs in this newspaper." He also placed a second large message, halfway through the newspaper, which said, "Stop counting, tell the experimenter you have seen this and win £250."

Overwhelmingly, the unlucky people completely missed the two large messages and just counted every photograph in the newspaper. This took them on average about two minutes to complete. Conversely, the vast majority of lucky people read both of the large messages, stopped counting, and completed the experiment within a matter of seconds.

After marrying his observations with various personality tests of the participants, Wiseman concluded that unlucky people are usually extremely anxious and tense. Research shows that anxiety inhibits a person's ability to notice anything that is unexpected. Anxious people tend to be consumed by their thoughts and unaware of anything unrelated to their worries. Unlucky people, therefore, miss chance opportunities because they are too busy looking for the things they are focused on.

In life, unlucky people will go to a party with the only focus of finding their perfect romantic partner. In doing so, they miss the opportunity to make new friends. Unlucky people will scour the internet with the sole focus of finding a specific kind of job and will miss information about a different kind of job that is better for them.

Wiseman found that lucky people are more relaxed and open. They will see what is in front of them, rather than just what they are looking for. They are more likely to make new friends at a party while also being open to a romantic relationship. They are more likely to notice an unexpected opportunity, leading to success, while also looking for a job on the internet. Lucky people, therefore, notice more things than unlucky people.

Additionally, Wiseman found that lucky people intentionally change the pattern of their behavior and in doing so maximize the chances of seeing new opportunities. They will often disrupt their normal routine, thus creating the possibility of chance encounters and new experiences. He found that lucky people did this without realizing they were doing it. The motivation to change their routine was often because they liked change and new experiences. As discussed earlier, embracing the unknown and being inspired by new things are both childhood traits.

To confirm his findings, Wiseman asked his volunteers to change their habits and to spend a month carrying out various exercises to enhance their luck. They were asked to keep an open mind and to look at the positive side of things, including the positive side of bad experiences. They were asked to alter their routine and to do things differently, such as change their route to work. They were also encouraged to trust their intuition.

After one month, 80 percent of the people in the research project reported that they were happier and luckier in life. The unlucky people had become lucky and the lucky people had become ever luckier.

A perceived obstacle to us expressing gratitude can sometimes be that we feel we have nothing to be grateful for. Actively adopting the traits of lucky people, as outlined previously, will increase our luck and the number of good things that we experience.

Key to this process, and a character trait of lucky people, is seeing the positive side in the face of adversity. Giving gratitude for our challenges can be immensely empowering. There really is a gift in every situation if we look at it in this way. It might be that we are learning new skills during challenging times, or that we discover an inner strength that we were previously unaware of. Or maybe the life challenge has also revealed something about a situation that we really needed to know.

Wiseman connects the ability to see the positive side of our challenges to a person's resilience. The more we see the positive things in negative situations, the more resilient we become. This is in contrast to a person seeing themselves only as a victim, which is a common trait of unlucky people.

Happily, we can increase our luck, both easily and relatively quickly. It is the same as receiving the rewards from expressing gratitude. If we want it, we can have it.

Act on the Ideas

"It [Gratitude] turns what we have into enough, and more. It turns denial into acceptance, chaos to order, confusion to clarity . . . Gratitude makes sense of our past, brings peace for today, and creates a vision for tomorrow."

MELODY BEATTIE

We know that expressing gratitude can help us physically, emotionally, and mentally. It can make us happier, improve our relationships, and bring us greater success. By expressing gratitude and making this a daily part of our lives, we can literally change our world.

This book is all about igniting our enthusiasm for life, uplifting our emotions, and opening the door to new opportunities. Embracing gratitude, if we are willing to do so, is the fast-track way to achieve this goal.

However, it doesn't end there. Trevor McKinney's plan in *Pay It Forward* was to change the world by paying good fortune forward and sharing it with others. Studies have shown that common traits of grateful people include wanting to do good deeds for others. They also tend to feel compassion for people and trust others more than ungrateful people do.

We can enhance these positive traits within ourselves by thinking about the people in our lives, our family, the people who we work with, and our friends. Now identify one positive quality about a selection of them. It might be a character trait that we admire, an action they have taken, or something that they have done for us. Feel gratitude for this favorable aspect of each of those people. Finally, we need to make a concerted effort to let them know how we feel about them. We might say:

I really appreciate how you are always there for me.

Thank you for helping me the other day.

*I really admire what you have
achieved with your work.*

Expressing gratitude for the people in our lives will boost our overall feeling of well-being, as well as increase the happiness of those around us. Over time, putting this idea into action will inevitably change each of our worlds for the better.

TOP TIPS

1. Write down any five things that you feel grateful for about your character traits and achievements.

2. Write down two things about three different people that you are thankful for. Tell those people why you feel grateful for them.

3. Repeat five positive affirmations about yourself in the mirror. Start with the examples in this chapter and then experiment with your own.

4. Give thanks for being alive!

5. Be thankful for what you have, rather than focusing on what you don't have.

6. Play with gratitude. Take things a little more lightly at times. Do this by engaging in an activity that you enjoy and find fun to perform. Express this in writing as a gratitude at the end of the experience.

7. Change your routine at least once a week.

8. Try to be more optimistic and expect the best even when you are experiencing challenges.

9. Doodle in your book.

AFTERWORD
INTO THE WILD

The battered old jeep hurtled along the narrow road, swerving at speed around cows, water buffaloes, and people. Makeshift homes and shops, fashioned from wooden poles and corrugated iron, lined each side of the street. The structures were interjected by long stretches of reeds and paddy fields, at which point the temperature outside would suddenly drop.

I had never before seen earth so red, or an early morning sky look so mesmerizing. A cosmic scene of indigos, pinks, and magentas arched across the horizon. These colors were punctuated by the lush green of the coconut palms, which appeared to grow everywhere.

The sensory overload was ramped up as I detected a myriad of tantalizing aromas from alluring cooking smells to the scent of the jungle and iron-rich earth. Exotic animals screeched and boomed above our heads. Vehicles honked their horns, and people called to one another from across the street. I couldn't wait to taste the food, explore the land, and meet its people.

Admittedly, I also thought that I might die. The driver, casually chatting on his mobile phone, hung out of the window to wave jovially at passers-by. I was certain that he was staring out of his window much longer than was safe to do so. How could he possibly see all of the oncoming obstacles, from livestock to people, trucks, cars, and motorbikes?

I could also see what looked like shrines to the dead. Garlands of flowers and photographs of the deceased were positioned on hairpin bends and at the roots of roadside trees. These were surely the victims of road traffic accidents. Regardless of what these were, if this was to be my last day on earth, I didn't care.

Just two months before, my first wife had died. And now, some friends of mine had invited me to their tropical home, thinking that it might help me and my boys in the aftermath of the death. I didn't know what I thought. I felt broken, lost, and emotionally raw. Until this point.

Living in England, with its buttoned-up approach to death, and its stifling regulations around safety, I found nothing that I could relate to. Nothing that could match the intensity of my experience of death on the magnitude that I was feeling it. I felt a cavernous disconnect between the reality that everyone is eventually going to die and the denial of death, which is prevalent within English culture. I wanted something massive to happen. Something that would meet the enormity of the feelings that consumed me . . . something real.

At last, at my most desperate point, I had found it. A place so magnificent in its beauty and authenticity that there was no option other than to be completely in the moment and in awe of everything that I could see. This was my first experience of India.

My sons and I would soon be exploring remote jungles, standing under crystal-clear waterfalls, and swimming in the warm Indian Ocean. We would eat fresh watermelon and mangoes, straight off the land, and drink milk from coconuts that we had cut by hand.

The people, the colors, and the tastes were all new to us. The regular sight of entire families, laden with groceries and precariously balanced on a single moped, was liberating to see. Everywhere we went and everything we encountered felt unique and bursting with energy. This was exactly the intensity I had been looking for.

In the wake of death and feeling betrayed by everything that I had spent a lifetime investing in, I found myself rejecting all of my previous beliefs and expectations. I had taken my rule book for life and thrown it away. However, instead of finding something awful with which to match my pain, I had now found a place so intense, so sensual, and so beautiful that it eclipsed it.

Discarding my usual beliefs and behaviors meant that there were not the usual cultural filters through which I viewed the world. And on top of that, I was now inhabiting a land so contrasting to my own, and so vivid on every level, that it felt completely wild, fresh, and new. It inspired a state of consciousness within me, close to that which I had experienced as a young child. It was as if the many layers of societal conditioning, which I had acquired through my education, parenting, the media, and wider society, had fallen away. I was now seeing and feeling things for the very first time. And instead of only feeling grief and disconnection, I felt the first flickers of connection again.

***

*"Very little is needed to make a happy life;
it is all within yourself, in your way of thinking."*
MARCUS AURELIUS, MEDITATION

It shouldn't require a trauma in life for us to expand our consciousness and to evolve. My first trip to India was immensely enlightening and enhanced my spirit of adventure, imagination, and playful nature, but it also felt incredibly sad. Since that time, and using the techniques described in this book, I have come to realize that adopting a more playful and adventurous outlook on life has the potential to promote self-development through joy, rather than through pain.

So much of living a more carefree existence, one that is imbued with play and adventure, is about giving ourselves permission to do so. It is a mindset, which is easily accessible if only we choose to embrace it. The "top tips" that we have been experimenting with and the freedom of thought that doodling can offer will assist us with this process. Playing around with new ways of behaving and thinking will loosen us up and make us more open to fresh ways of living.

Adopting some of the top tips, whether to increase our access to flow, making gratitude a regular part of our lives, breaking the rules, or building resilience, will help us to discover our numerous inner resources and attributes, both currently known and unknown.

My years of teaching young children, raising my children, and reflecting on my own childhood has inspired me to examine the seemingly magical realms of a child. I spent years writing down my thoughts on this subject—rough notes on loose pieces of paper and longer prose in journals. If I couldn't find the right words for my thoughts, I would doodle instead. Random drawings and abstract images, finished and unfinished, became part of my regular thought process. I found that the act of doodling loosens up the mind and allows various insights to emerge from unexpected places. These collections of thoughts and my research into the mechanics of the imagination and play then evolved into this book, which you are now holding.

Throughout this book, we have explored a variety of clear ways with which we can successfully tap into childhood traits. The numerous benefits, such as leading a happier life, are accessible to us all. We just need to know that we can get to that uplifting place from here, where we are right now, no matter how life might currently appear. After all, the only way is up from the bottom.

It was during my first trip to India that I met Sundeep, a beautiful Punjabi Indian woman, who I would later form a romantic relationship with and marry. We would go on to share a desire for adventure together and strive for a more playful existence, living our life with our two boys, Iggy and Tali, and twin daughters, Luna and Star. I would never have predicted this outcome from the emotional place I inhabited while in India all those years ago.

Imagination and the childhood traits of play and adventure are our allies. We don't have to know precisely where we are heading, but embracing these precious inner qualities will make life's journey a more joyous one. Living the life of our dreams then becomes not only desirable, but also inevitable.

***

"It's never too late to have a happy childhood."
TOM ROBBINS, *STILL LIFE WITH WOODPECKER*

Two weeks into our trip to India, I found myself deep within the heart of a jungle. We had gone to see a famous banyan tree that we had heard about from our friends. I had grown up with thousand-year-old oaks, and even older yew trees, in the woodlands of my childhood, so I have always had a fascination with ancient trees. The banyan tree is not as old as some of the trees native to Britain, but is usually much bigger and certainly hundreds of years old.

I explored the banyan tree's enormous branches and climbed inside its hollow center, just as I had entered the hollow trunks of yews as a child. I put my hands on the bark and felt its large leathery leaves. Unlike the remote trees of my childhood, where I would be the only person in sight, this tree had holy men sitting at its roots, burning incense, and performing ceremonies. There were necklaces, feathers, and other ritual items tied to its low-hanging branches. The environment had an air of sacredness and mysticism about it, which felt enticing.

Making our way down from the hill, on which the banyan was growing, my sons and I walked through the jungle and on to a less trodden and more hidden path. The afternoon sun was extremely hot, so we were grateful for the shade from the trees and other foliage that surrounded us. Everything felt exotic about this place. We would suddenly duck as unfamiliar and extremely large insects flew past our heads. Snakes slid by in the long reeds and monkeys leapt in the trees above our heads. Again, the feeling was reminiscent of my childhood adventures, but instead of imagining that I was in a jungle, with its dangerous animals and strange sounds, here I was discovering a real one. There was a sense of trepidation, as well as intense excitement. We had no idea where we were, where we were going, or what we would find. And the three of us were loving every bit of it.

Eventually, we came across a river. At first, we heard it and changed our course to investigate the sound. A fast-flowing, ice-cold channel of water cascaded down the hillside. It felt like this adventure was becoming more breathtaking and sensational with every step. As soon as we were able to, we threw off our clothes and submerged ourselves in the water.

The rivers and lakes that I had discovered as a child came rushing back to my memory. Now, just as before, the brisk shock to the system as we entered the water forced us into the present moment. We all gasped, shouted, and laughed.

Pressing on, our clothes draped over our shoulders, we continued to walk through the jungle and followed the course of the river downhill. The foliage was extremely dense and impenetrable in places, so the river was the only route that we could take. To our delight, around a bend, the water dropped off very suddenly and we found ourselves at the top of a waterfall. It was roughly 20 feet to the ground with huge boulders on either side, which we used to help us climb and slide down to its base.

This was one of those occasions when I have experienced the state of consciousness known as flow. We were completely lost in the present moment; our physical skills were being sufficiently tested and everything felt timeless and connected. What felt like minutes in this place turned out to be hours.

On reaching the foot of the waterfall, we cast our clothes to one side and dived into the water again. We positioned our heads directly under the waterfall, so that it pummeled us from above. The urge to play and to explore was utterly irresistible. My sons, Tali and Iggy, laughed and played in the water, jumping in and out of the icy pool and finding new ways to explore the terrain.

In the heat of the sun and warming myself up again on a large boulder, I watched my boys continue to play in the water. I reflected again on my own childhood and remembered the places that I had discovered as a child, the times when I had got lost, the feelings of excitement, and the way in which my imagination would run wild. It was as if I had traveled back in time and was experiencing those feelings all over again. A sense of *déjà vu* dawned on me.

Then, shouting out a warrior cry, I leapt over the boulders and the bodies of my children and dived back into the water. The call to play was within me. I felt alive . . . like a wild thing.

In many ways, this time in my life was the turning point for me to amalgamate all that I had learnt from my childhood and from my work with children in education and apply those lessons to myself. From that moment on, I committed to a life of adventure and play.

"So many people live within unhappy circumstances and yet will not take the initiative to change their situation because they are conditioned to a life of security, conformity, and conservatism, all of which may appear to give one peace of mind, but in reality nothing is more damaging to the adventurous spirit within a man than a secure future."

CHRISTOPHER MCCANDLESS, *INTO THE WILD*

Do you remember how adventurous life was when you were a child and the freedom you experienced then? Do you remember those times when there were no adults about, when no one was telling you what to do, when you climbed trees, built camps, became an adventurer, and looked out on a world of unlimited possibilities? Like your favorite characters in books and on TV shows, you felt like the master of your own destiny and always on the verge of discovering pots of gold and treasure maps. And do you remember going home after the day was done, the feeling of greatness inside you, your experiences and thoughts and a kind of fulfillment all fizzing inside? You felt free. You felt complete.

How come it went away?

For some of us, we left this magical world during our teen years or early adulthood. It probably got drummed out of us by our parents, peers, and school. We then acquired a more serious outlook on life, complete with a set of self-imposed limitations and rules. The exciting characters we once imagined ourselves to be were replaced by our "sensible" reasons for not being them. The pots of gold and the treasure maps gradually slipped out of sight, and our sense of freedom and limitlessness disappeared.

This book is about reclaiming these things and much more.

Throughout this book, we have rekindled our enthusiasm for life's adventure as a means to leading a happier, healthier, and more exciting existence. We have evoked the playful spirit of childhood that we once enjoyed, discovering buried treasure along the way. We have explored how being more imaginative, carefree, maverick, and risk-taking enhances our relationships, our work, and our leisure time. Moreover, we have also learnt how adopting a more adventurous and playful attitude to life can lead us toward a more stress-free life and help us to access a deeper sense of well-being.

Let us not wait any longer to embrace our birthright to feel happy and excited about life. The techniques to achieve this are quite simple if we are open and willing to use them.

Ultimately, this book shows us that our childhood sense of possibility never really disappeared; it was simply out of sight for a short while and is now waiting for us to rediscover it. It is an invitation for us to be playful. To be wild things. To be free.

ABOUT THE AUTHOR

Russell Sach

Mike Fairclough is an internationally acclaimed educator, with over 25 years' experience in the field. Throughout this time, he has been at the forefront of character education and developed an approach to self-development that embraces risk-taking, the concept of people moving out of their comfort zones, and the building of grit and resilience.

As an integral part of the school he leads, Mike also runs a farm, which includes a herd a water buffalo, beekeeping, and outdoor learning. His television appearances, press coverage, and writing on the subject of character building have helped shape the education landscape and empower children and adults alike. Mike lives on rural England's south coast with his wife and four children.

www.mikefairclough.squarespace.com

HAY HOUSE

Look within

Join the conversation about latest products,
events, exclusive offers and more.

f Hay House

  @HayHouseUK

 @hayhouseuk

 healyourlife.com

We'd love to hear from you!